SWING TRADING

The Final Guide to Improve Your Beginner Strategies,

Make Your Risk Management More Efficient

and Achieve A Passive Income Investing Day by Day

on Forex, Stocks and Options Market.

By

Ryan Drake

© Copyright 2020 by Ryan Drake

All rights reserved.

This document is geared towards providing exact and reliable information in regards to the topic and issue covered. The publication is sold with the idea that the publisher is not required to render accounting, officially permitted, or otherwise, qualified services. If advice is necessary, legal or professional, a practiced individual in the profession should be ordered. - From a Declaration of Principles which was accepted and approved equally by a Committee of the American Bar Association and a Committee of Publishers and Associations. In no way is it legal to reproduce, duplicate, or transmit any part of this document in either electronic means or in printed format. Recording of this publication is strictly prohibited and any storage of this document is not allowed unless with written permission from the publisher. All rights reserved. The information provided herein is stated to be truthful and consistent, in that any liability, in terms of inattention or otherwise, by any usage or abuse of any policies, processes, or directions contained within is the solitary and utter responsibility of the recipient reader. Under no circumstances will any legal responsibility or blame be held against the publisher for any reparation, damages, or monetary loss due to the information herein, either directly or indirectly. Respective authors own all copyrights not held by the publisher. The information herein is offered for informational purposes solely and is universal as so. The presentation of the information is without a contract or any type of guarantee assurance. The trademarks that are used are without any consent, and the publication of the trademark is without permission or backing by the trademark owner. All trademarks and brands within this book are for clarifying purposes only and are owned by the owners themselves, not affiliated with this document.

TABLE OF CONTENTS

Introduction 5

Chapter 1: How Trading Works 8

Chapter 2: How Swing Trading Works 14

Chapter 3: Swing Trading Against Position Trading 23

Chapter 4: Swing Trading Against Day Trading 28

Chapter 5: Choose The Instruments 41

Chapter 6: Tools And Platforms For Swing Trading 79

Chapter 7: Fundamental Analysis 88

Chapter 8: Technical Analysis 95

Chapter 9: Risk Management 103

Chapter 10: The Skill You Need Yo Achieve Your Financial Income 168

Chapter 11: How To Find Transitions In Swing Trading 175

Chapter 12: 10 Entry Strategies 182

Chapter 13: 10 Exit Strategies 189

Chapter 14: What You Will Never Have To Do – The Big Mistakes 196

Chapter 15: A Success Story 202

Chapter 16: A Story Of Ruin 207

Conclusion 212

INTRODUCTION

On the continuum of trading stock, swing trading sits in between day trading and trend trading. To better understand it, you first have to understand what day trading and trend trading are.

• A day trader holds a stock for a short amount of time, it can be hours and never more than a day, before they trade it.

• A trend trader, on the other hand, looks at the behaviour of a stock and at its long-term patterns, he monitors the relative index and hold on to it for weeks, even months, before they trade.

Now, whatever these two styles represent in your mind – swing trading is in between.

In this book I am going to guide you through practical approaches to swing trading, through the basics and the Nitti gritty that you need to know in order to earn consistently as a swing trader. This is not going to be just a common-sense guide, but we will go through tested and proven principles that will lead you to the top.

Teaching about swing trading is one thing, but you learning it is another.

What do I mean? First, you have to learn the principles I will be sharing with you, examine and make them yours and then use them to your personal needs.

We will start from the ABC of how swing trading works; then we will examine the best trading instrument that will suit you and your lifestyle (it is best to choose instruments you understand the most). Later we will have a look at tools and platforms for swing trading and finally we will learn the fundamentals and technical analysis.

An important aspect we will touch is 'risk management' : you need to take the right amount of risk for every stage you are in. We will look at: the skills needed in swing trading to achieve financial income, how to find transitions, entry and exit strategies, big mistakes that you should never make and some real-life stories of success and loss.

Do you want to make money with swing trading? Move on to the next sections and start learning.

CHAPTER 1
HOW TRADING WORKS

The internet has unlocked a lot of knowledge that otherwise would have probably been kept only for the elite. Almost everyone has access to internet now and many different things can be learnt and done with it. Things like programming, web design, graphic design, even learning how to cook can be learnt now for free and remotely; this would have been impossible decades ago.

The same can be said about how to make money

Online trading has become extremely popular since we can buy and sell shares/stocks, we can become brokers and we can invest money from a laptop, all thanks to internet.

Online trading is simply the act of purchasing and selling products on the internet, as easy as that. It is totally similar to physical trading, where you want something and you have the money for it, so you buy it.

The only difference is that you do not physically meet the buyer or the seller.

Sometimes, you may not have the exact amount of money to make a trade or transaction, this is where a broker comes in. He is that person (or company) who has money and is willing to partner with you. The investor does not need to meet the broker, they could be in different parts of the world and still have the business go on smoothly, they may not even know each other.

Here are some of the requirements for online trading

Savings account: As long as it has to be an online trade, there will be a place where the money will be debited from or credited to, that is your personal account, 'the saving account' . You cannot have an online transaction without having a savings account, this is where the money will be sent from, as well as received.

Demat account: For you to have a smooth online transaction, you have to stay secure while online. The demat account houses the compilation of your financial securities online.

Trading account: The trading account is not your savings account; they are quite different. This is the account that brokerage company gives to you in order for you to make your transactions.

Trading platform: This is the platform where you will make your trade, check prices etc.. In here you will be able to buy or sell whatever stock you want.

The advisor: This advisor is provided by the brokerage firm and is responsible for guiding you in the right path, in order to make beneficial decisions.

The communication between all of the above takes you to online trading. These are the basics of what online trading involves.

Here's how it works, for you to trade online as an

"ordinary" individual (by ordinary, I mean you do not run any company) you have to choose an online broker. He is the one that take care of the deals and keeps your money in an account – the trading account. There are lots of firms to choose from and, based on the account and the package we choose, we get different levels of help. Before making your choice, carefully inform yourself between the options you have.

There are a few things you must take in consideration while you go on with your research of a broker.

Money

How much do you want to invest? Most firms have a minimum amount for each trade and some also have a standard deposit to open an account. You must know how much you're willing to invest.

Frequency

How frequently would you buy stock? Would you just get one or two and hold on to them long term? Would you buy as many as you can? This is important so you will be able to know how much a broker will charge you.

To be able to trade, you must have an account.

Assuming you want to open an account with an online brokerage in the United States of America, you will be asked questions about your finances, how much you have and if the amount in question would be enough for what you are about to get into. As for investments you are not financially buoyant to handle, the brokerages would not let you go on with the application. Your personal details like your cell phone number, address will be required so that your investments and progress will be adequately tracked.

After you have been able to create your account, you will be able trade. Before that, a real-time stock quote is necessary. Most of brokerages firm come with this option. Some free financial sites, instead, would present with delayed quotes, these ones are behind the market, at least by twenty minutes. If you are in a fast market and you only depend on delayed quotes, you will be in trouble since all the information turn out to be wrong.

Whenever you decide to make a trade, place a market order or a limit order.

The current market price of the stock is where the market order operates. A limit order would be preferable, you set a limit on the price you're willing to pay, if the price doesn't reach this limit, the order won't go through.

Stop orders, trailing stop orders, stop limit orders.

All these are different orders which can be issued on your trade for it to be stopped when the market prices are falling.

It is important to understand that online trading does not happen at the instant the command is issued; let's say you are placing a market order, it takes time to find a seller or even a buyer, and also to process the trade It goes through when the markets are open.

CHAPTER 2
HOW SWING TRADING WORKS

Before we can figure out how the swing trading works, we must first understand that there are different trading time frames and it is essential to understand them.

Squeezing profit from the markets can be easy to an extent, because the market where these things occur is really a large one. Other than several trading strategies, there are also different trading styles. A major variant in the style to use, is the time frame you trade in.

On one side, there are brokers who practice long-term trading. They watch the trends for much longer periods, for months or even years.

There are opportunities to have large profits but, at the same time, just like any other business, you may occur in losses. Long-term trading could surpass what can be achieved within a shorter period. Moreover, the attention which would be given to long trades will be less, as they would just be monitored once in a while each day.

On the other side, there are the scalpers. They make really short-term trades; sometimes, these trades last for only a few minutes. They simply trade for a few minutes and are comfortable with whatever they end with, then they close the trade for that day.

When you work with those short lengths trades, you would be able to cut down the rate at which you are opened to the market, plus at this level, you work just with small price movements.

Everything on earth has its advantages and disadvantages, so does the scalping. Some of its disadvantages include: it takes a lot of attention as well as time; you must give it the best you can so that you are not caught unawares, you must be thorough with your exit management - this one must be top-notch.

Furthermore, we have day traders: these ones can

keep trading for as long as they want to, but no more than one day. This way, they also avoid being exposed to stories on the market which may be favourable or unfavourable.

Between these categories sits swing trading. The trades, with this style, can last from few days to few weeks. The "swing traders" looks for multiple day chart patterns to log on to because these ones would have bigger price moves; they would even be able to get in more than one per day – as per day trading. Thus, it is better to swing trade than to day trade.

Many people find this style very appealing because it offers an acceptable compromise between the frequency of trades and the associated time demands.

Generally, as a swing trader, it is expected that you work on four-hour (H4) and daily (D1c) charts alongside your fundamental and technical analysis, which help you in making the right decisions.

For a swing trader, volatility is the key. This is because

there is an increase in the number of short-term price movements and once a swing trader understands this, he is set out to have the best times.

Some advantages

Time

Just like I stated before, the short-term trades need to be checked regularly while long term trades don't.

One of the reasons most people would switch to swing trading is because it uses a friendly time-frame. Swing traders spend less time on analysis and spend even less time in a day in making trades

The longer trends

Other types or forms of trading, like scalping, rely on short-term volatility, but swing trading lets traders to be able to maximize the open window in longer term trades. There may be false signals on short-term trading, while those which are longer could be much reliable.

Another advantage of swing trading is that its time units allow you to get the best out of the simplest indicators.

Take for example a daily candlestick closing above the 40-period MA (moving average). If this same candlestick was on a 5-minute chart, it would be much shorter and less accurate, but more accurate results could be gotten over longer time frames.

In swing trading, you must have a plan. Without it, you would end up making mistakes you may not even be aware of. If you do not measure progress, you would not be able to grow.

Swing trading works by knowing what, how and when to trade. You must carefully choose your trading style and strategy and all these things have to be included in your plan.

Swing trading is possible on all kinds of markets, including stocks, forex, indices etc.

Timeframe

You may be wondering what the best time frame is, but the truth is that there is no best timeframe, it depends on the trends and the time it would take for it to be actualized.

In swing trading with forex, there are different choices for your strategy: there is following the trend or trading counter to the trend.

For both of them, the ability to notice the price action, that is the price movement in the chart, is important.

Following the trend (Trend trading)

Markets do not move in a straight line, they go up and down, never straight. By the market setting higher highs and lows, we can notice the uptrend, while a low trend can be noticed by having lower lows and highs. Swing trading strategies look out for and try to catch a short trend.

Look at this daily chart of EUR / USD.

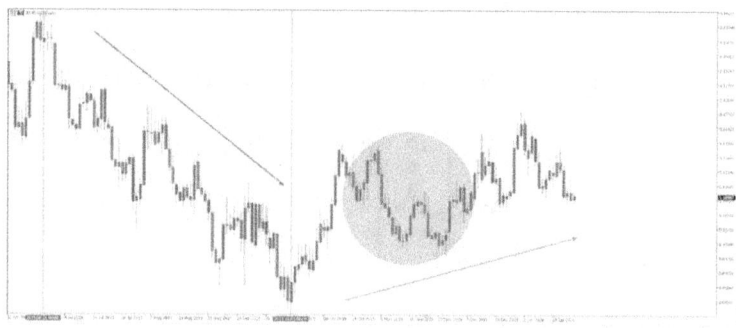

Source: EURUSD, Chart D1, MT5 Admiral Markets. Data range: June 12, 2019 to January 22, 2020. Taken on January 22, 2020. Please note that past performance is not a reliable indicator of future results..

Look at that zigzag pattern, the Japanese candlestick here, this is typical of a downtrend which would last for about 3 months.

This trend is bullish, in October 2019, an upward trend ensues with high lows, but look at the section within the circle, a reversal takes place. At this point, while lows are falling, there is no new high being set. The uptrend continues after this period and goes up against the main trend.

When we are set the bullish trend will continue, then we go ahead to catch it using this simple trading method.

We must be sure the market would go back to its original trend before we engage, this means we must

- Go in search of a trend
- Then wait for a countertrend
- Once you notice the countertrend is over, you can now return to the market.

In this situation, all we are looking for is to see is that the market is on higher lows. In this case, no limit is set because there is no certainty to when the trend might end, there is also no certainty to the route the market may take, and there is no assurance to how high the market could go, hence, we do not set any price target.

You must wait, look and let the market digress to an extent.

In simple terms, swing trade works by knowing when

to get into a trade based on two types of swing: the high swing and the low swing.

The high swing refers to periods when the prices are really high while the low swing refers to periods when the prices are really low.

The swing trader tries to make the best off these movements between highs and lows. Going short (selling) is what traders do during downtrends while going long (buying) is what traders do during uptrends.

The aim is to get as much as can be taken form the price movements, because it is quite a hard task to determine the exact high and low of every movement.

CHAPTER 3
SWING TRADING AGAINST POSITION TRADING

The goal is to make profit and there are different ways of doing this. As a trader, you must be in the know or else you would slowly be kicked out, and lose a lot of money.

There are various strategies which every investor can use, depending on what is being traded. There are strategies which could be of great benefit when compared to others.

Position trading and swing trading all allow traders to move within the market - by move, I mean it allows them to trade better, depending on how skilled they are.

It should be noted that online trading should not be done just for fun, while you may be in it for fun, every other person is in it to make profit. If you are not consistent with what is going on in the market, you may eventually lose everything you put in.

While position trading involves holding an asset for a longer period of time, swing trading involves buying and selling assets frequently to take advantage of the price fluctuations.

Swing trading

Different positions could be plugged into (entered) and left just within a given period no longer than 3 weeks. It is a slower trading strategy compared to day trading.

Swing traders, look out for highs and lows in the assets price. With the information they get form that, they are able to forecast and determine the movement of prices which can be used to garner profit.

There is no guarantee that the events of the past would be exactly repeated in the present or future, swing traders still have to work with historical information to determine the best path to take.

When the market is static swing trading is in full force. In such markets, prices rise and fall in wave-like patterns, instead of having upward or downward trends (bullish or bearish trends). Whenever the market moves into either of these positions, swing trading becomes less effective, this is because moving in a particular direction can rattle the type of swing behaviour seen in trading periods which are less active

Position trading

For position trading, a stock is held for a longer period of time, over several weeks. news about the movement and fluctuations in the daily price does not influence position traders' strategy. They are focused on what happens in the long run. They allow whatever influence the fluctuations would have to just occur; instead of going long and going short in-between, they just stay focus on the outcome they have planned to achieve in the long run.

In picking stocks, position trading involves picking those that are forecasted to grow over a long period. They do this by following historical patterns and using tools like the fundamental and technical analysis tool.

Long term trend markers are used by position traders. If you do not have plans to become a position trader, it is better you stick with shirt term markers.

In my opinion, choosing a specific trading style is important and should be made considering both short and long-term goals. If as a trader, according to your speculations, there would be a volatile price of assets over a short period of time, maybe 2 weeks, it would be pertinent to choose a short-term position at that period instead of a long one

If you are looking to have something for yourself when you retire and you are looking to start online trading, it is best for you to explore various position trading options. The reason is that, since time is still on your side, you do not have to wait for short openings to make a move and keep watching that move, you can easily trade long term.

If you are going to be a professional trader, position trading is a no-no for you. You have all the time in the world to stay and "work" since this would be your main source of income.

If you are going to buy a specific stock shares, you must know the exact trading plan you need for that asset. You should know whether you need to hold the stock for days, hours, or even weeks or not. This will definitely help you.

CHAPTER 4
SWING TRADING AGAINST DAY TRADING

Sometimes, people make the mistake of thinking day trading is equal to investing, but this is not so. Day trading is not investing. The process of Investing involves buying shares or stakes in/of an asset for which there would be an increase in profit with time. The length of time is subjective, it could take years, or decades. Investors pay much attention to companies which they believe would have a great turnout in,

Day trading simply deals with buying and selling everything that day, all it takes is a few hours.

The pattern is the same as for investing but the time frame is different: they buy low and sell high, and they do this within a very small time of 24 hours. Taking advantage of very small price fluctuations, this is done, most of the time, with borrowed money

For example: a trader buys about 1500 shares of a stock at 11:00a.m. At 11:20am, the price begins to rise, and he sells. The day trader would make 500 dollars if the stock increases by half, this would be excluding commission. Depending on the platform that has been used.

An investment which you have had for less than a year will be taxed at a personal gain rate and this could go as high as 30 percent. For long term gains, they do not get up to that percentage. This means that taxing is a very important factor which should be carefully looked into when it comes to day trading.

From the example, it may look that the amount we just got is too small, but day traders do not make 3 or 5 transactions in a day, they make over 30. Profit can be multiplied when they increase the number of trades they make. Stock are not owned overnight because the market could easily fluctuate, with price changes falling or increasing drastically and traders must pay close attention to the news and corporate announcements which often drive the market.

Day traders move very fast, they do not wait, unlike investors who take their time to plan out the next moves to make or wait for additional information concerning the market. These day traders make moves even in seconds just to meet up and not be left behind

We have already discussed swing trading as well as position trading. It is important to note that day trading is the riskiest form, this is because you must be at alert as long as you want to trade.

Day traders must be smart and fast; they must know what to do at every point in time that day

It's easy to say you will do something, but it's harder to actually do it, especially when you are just learning it.

Day traders require the right skill, temperament, and even emotional intelligence. Here are some of the requirements they would need.

The basics

Knowledge - For you to succeed as a day trader, you must be familiar with what the market is about; it must be something easily accessible to you. You must be able to go through rigorous fronts to stay ahead. Having a wide experience base, due to years of investing, is very necessary

Capital - once day-traders are able to use a large amount of capital for smaller trades they would make smaller trades to have an increase in potential returns

The plan - Having a business plan can never be overemphasized; business plans tell what the trader would like to achieve in both short and long run. It includes trading markets, trading hours, the business setup needs, tax considerations etc. Without the plan, it would be quite difficult to make progress.

Discipline - Those who are day traders have to master the art of emotional intelligence, they must know how not to act on impulse, but take calculated steps in whatever deals they want to close. They must stick to working only with capital risks and know when to use their stop and limit orders.

Technology - This is the basis upon which all others exist, if you have no access to the needed equipment, there is no way you would be able to trade effectively and efficiently. A laptop/computer is the basic as well as high-speed internet connection, since all you need to ever do is to be over the web. For some people, all they need is their laptop; a high end one oftentimes. Others may need a set up with two monitors, where one would serve as a backup, but either way, having the necessary equipment is important.

Some persons who start day trading without having the right equipment may eventually get frustrated because all their expectations would not be met, they would be "late" to everything; for instance, their internet connection is not so good and they may have problems logging in into their account, not being able to make any trade. In a day trader world, every second and every minute counts, since, unlike position traders or swing traders, they have just 24 hours, or less (because they would have to sleep and do some other things for themselves), to make at least 20 trades.

Once some level of experience has been earned, some people, sometimes, may decide to become professional traders, because of the nature of the job. They could either work together by setting up with others or they could just work on their own.

Working as a part time trader is difficult, it's not that it's not possible but it's just difficult.

As a part time day trader, you must be committed as well as disciplined. They must religiously follow their routines

What most of day traders do is to pick out a particular market or two to trade in. When they know this market, they get familiar with all the nuances attached to the market, therefore with timing, and, as they build experience, they would know what to expect from most situations in the market.

Let's look into some of the popular markets for day traders and see how they are run. Popular markets for day traders include Stocks, Forex and futures

Futures

This happens when a trader decide to make a trade, i.e to buy and sell at a specific time and price in the future. Most of the futures contracts involve commodities used to trade which include textiles, fibers, metals, steer hides, rubbers etc.

Let's say you are a cocoa farmer and it's almost time to harvest some of your plants. You could sell your cocoa today and earn 10$, but you haven't harvested your cocoa yet, and you do not know exactly if the prices would fall or rise; if they rise, you would gain a lot but if they fall, you would be knocked out. So, you could look for someone who is willing to buy, maybe someone that processes cocoa and converts it to chocolates. You sign a futures contract with that person, agreeing to sell a specific amount of cocoa at a specific date later in the future and you negotiate at a price to sell one for 9.5$. if you eventually get to harvest your cocoa and, at the point of you selling it, the price is 8$, you have lost money but you have made money over the futures price. If at the point of selling, the price is still 10$, you have made a loss but you can still made up for that loss by selling your cocoa as you regularly would.

For the day trader who works on futures, the same principle as the above example applies to him, unless there are certain changes in some of the index. He practically hopes and believes that at a certain date in the future, there would be an increase in the prices of commodities, hence he would be able to make some profit

Forex

Forex is simply getting some sort of income from fluctuations in the exchange rates of different currencies. It is a large market with loads of opportunities and is open 6 days in a week. Traders who run day trades must use leverage as a tool in order to make maximum profit.

Stock market

Stock market is also very popular, the same theory applies as to the case of forex, everyone wants it where it is big. The NASDAQ has more companies than the New York Stock Exchange and as a result of this, most people flock to the NASDAQ exchange. The market is totally volatile because the companies are relatively small and focused on products which have to do with technology. Traders as a result of these factors are able to get a lot of opportunities.

In looking for the best market which would suit you, you must look out for:

Volatility. It measure how much the price of a commodity will vary over time. There are lots of fluctuations going on with the prices of highly volatile securities, and this makes it a key target for day traders since it is where there are day price movements to profit from.

Liquidity. Is simply the ability to trade an asset without affecting its pricing levels. Such assets experience a lot of trading activity, this is because as long as the pricing levels are not affected, they can be traded several times in a day.

I have mentioned earlier that a strategy used by day traders work with is leveraging. Here's how it works: let's say that a certain trade could bring you to have a 5 percent return; If you have $20,000 sitting in your account then your return would be $1000 but, assuming you borrow an extra $20,000 and add them to your current money, your return would be $2,000 – you have doubled your returns. With leverage, you would be able to increase the money which comes into your coffers without increasing the trade's performance

Day traders' strategies

Leveraging and selling short

In order for leveraging to work, the trader need to borrow money; most people take them from their brokerage firms by using the margin account. Once a margin account has been opened, about 50 percent of the selling price of a stock can be borrowed. This is what is referred to as buying on margin.

In selling short, a trader has to borrow a security and sell it in the market planning to buy it back later on, at a reduced price. Here, the practice of buying low and selling high is ignored, the trader bet on the dropping of security's price.

- Makes a move to sell the stock i.e he places an order to do so
- He tells his broker he wants to borrow them, he does not own them
- Allows the firm borrow the share then give it to him as a loan and then he places it on that the

stock should be sold

- When there is a reduction in selling price then he proceeds to buy the share in the market
- Gets back to the broker to pay back the loan which he incurred
- There would definitely be a difference which would be left, this would be his profit

Both strategies actually take on a lot of risks, sometimes, the market won't turn out the way the traders thought, hence, the money that have already been borrowed as leverage would need to be refunded. There is also a loophole, really common, known as the margin call; whenever the value of a margin account falls below what is expected, that is the maintenance margin, the trader must deposit more money into the account. If the trader cannot deposit money, then the broker would have to sell off the securities of the trader until that maintenance margin is attained again. To avoid this, day traders must use stop-losses and they must be effective at using them. A stop loss order works by ordering the sell of a security at the market price that has been attained immediately when hits a certain level.

Should you go on and become a day trader as opposed to being a swing trader? The choice is up to you, you must first know what you hope to achieve from the market, and then consider certain factors like how much time you have to spare, would you be going professional or would it be a part time job etc. you could use some of the pointers I have already outlined in this book to fix that for yourself.

CHAPTER 5
CHOOSE THE INSTRUMENTS

There are several financial instruments for swing trading. Which one to use depend on the trader, his experience, how much risk he is willing to take and manage and on the market conditions at the time of the trade. Choosing an instrument also involves considering the advantages and the disadvantages of each one of them and deciding which works best for the trader.

FOREX

Forex trading styles can be separated according to the amount of time a trader expects a winning trade to last for. This will determine the actions taken by the trader for the trade, using the time frame for their chart and for the implementation of the required trading tools and risk management techniques. Another factor that is important to consider is the amount of time you have to spare for your trade. The good news is, no matter how much or little time the trader might have, there is a trading style that suits his needs.

It is good to note that this flexibility doesn't mean that forex trading is easier and don' t require knowledge. For example: Scalping is considered the shortest startegy. Their entire focus is to get very small profits. The trade lasts for a short period, a few minutes or hours. The main idea is for the small trades to accumulate into a good profit. This is highly advantageous for people with full time jobs or commitments that take a large part of their day. Now, this is great, trading for a short time and making profit, but this doesn't make it less problematic. In fact, because of the short length it requires as much or even more planning than the other strategies.

Every small detail must be noted in order to avoid mistakes, this is why it is highly recommended that Scalping be carried out by those with forex trading experience, or a general level of expertise. The market can be overwhelming for a person with no experience, especially with the short frame of time that requires an exit plan and risk management. Scalping shows that as much as the time frame is short, and leaves room for other life pursuits, it is as tasking as every other strategy. Forex trading needs work and a high level of commitment even if it might be just for a few minutes or hours. There are other fast forex trading strategies, like day trading, where the time frame is a bit longer than for the scalpers. They hold their trade for a day without keeping it overnight. Day traders have more breathing room but this doesn't mean less work. It takes the same energy and mastery that Scalping requires.

There is the long-term trading, this is everything Scalping and day trading isn't in relation to time and volatility. Long term traders, as the name implies, can hold a position for longer periods, from weeks to months. This wouldn't give the trader so much time for a full-time job, but it brings a level of stability and peace. The volatility of the charts and how they fluctuate won't affect the trader much. This strategy has the time on its side, something that the first two aforementioned strategies do not have, so traders can move at a steady pace till they attain their goals.

It is easier to spot an imminent loss and gather the already made profit. As appealing as this type of forex trading strategy is, it is important to note that it would only work for those whose major source of income is from forex trading. Simply put, the benefits from this trading strategy is like its name goes - long term. So, if the results needed are immediate, go for a short-term approach.

Swing trading is between day trading and long-term trading. They are not limited by the constraints of time; a position can remain open for few weeks. The focus is usually the swing: the fluctuations that causes the highs or the lows. These movements are key to the trader's profit. Simply put: a trader spots the trend, waits for retracement and then makes profit as the trend moves. This isn't restricted to uptrends alone, in forex both direction (uptrends and downtrends) can yield good profit. Swing trading is centered on paying close attention to time frames, putting together different analysis (technical, sentimental, fundamental) and also focuses on how volatile the market is at different times.

Here are a few terminologies used in forex trading and their definitions

- Exchange rate: this refers to the rate for which one currency is exchanged for another. The rate tells you how much the currency is per unit.

- Ask price: this is also called the offer price. This is the price you can buy the instrument being traded at the set time

- Bid price: this is the price you can sell the currency for or the instrument being traded at the set time.

- Pip: this refers to the small price change in a given exchange rate.
- Spread: this is the difference between the purchase price and the sale price offered.
- Pip Value: this refers to the value of 1 pip. This changes with the market movements.
- Entry: this is when a trader opens a position by buying or selling.
- Exit: this is when market position is closed either with a profit or with a loss.
- A bull: a bull is a trader that believes in the upward movement of the market. The person is usually described as being bullish
- A bear: a bear is the opposite of a bull. He believes the market would fall. In this case the person is usually described as bearish.
- Long positions: this refers to entering a buy position.

- Leverage: This refers to the amount of money deposit you need for a given transaction.

- Margins: this refers to the amount of money you need to have with a broker to make a forex trade especially for a certain amount.

Advantages

- Time management: Forex swing trading takes less time for the completion of all the related tasks: analysis, risk management and trading. This trade requires more observation than hands on activity. Though the long-term traders have time as an advantage too, they put in a lot more mental effort into correctly analyzing the future of the market; this is definitely more stressful that a few minutes of trading the forex swing traders put in per trade.

- Has various support instruments: this trading allows the use of a wide range of supporting tools and they have these instruments at their disposal, mostly because of their time frames.

- Saves Costs: the processes of trading can be expensive no matter the strategy used and this does not include the starting investment and the swap (overnight) charges. Forex traders hardly go through the hassle of spread. In some strategies the spread charged is usually more than the profit made. Forex swing traders don't go through this because the trade is stretched between two prices. Spread is charged every time a trade is completed and it is the difference between the ask price and the bid price.

Disadvantages

- The learning: this is a disadvantage for some traders, especially new ones who just want to get into trading. If profit is going to be made from forex swing trading, the process has to be learnt. The strategies, the planning and all the process may appear easy, but, in order to handle complications on the go, you need to get familiar with all the possible hassles and risks that may arise. One of the best ways to practice and learn is to set up a demo account. This gives room to experiment and try out different strategies and the combinations that yield actual profit.

- External factors: Forex trading most of the time can be affected by factors beyond the trader's controls. This doesn't change the fact that the forex market is driven by traders but many times economic and political factors may affect the forex market. This is one of the biggest troubles of forex swing trading, because traders may be profiting one moment and then wake up the next and an economical change they had no control of, may turn their profits into a loss. Usually, there is always a slim chance for the traders to withdraw.

- Swap Fee: this doesn't mean much to those traders that leave their positions open for a day. This is heavy for those that carry their open positions over to the next day. The fees may differ according to the current market price and sometimes it may be fixed. When swings take time to get to the point, usually means that swap fees increases and it is usually charged from the traders account.

STOCKS

Stocks swing trading involves buying and selling of stock with the only intention of holding the position for days, or weeks in a few cases. Many traders follow the largely used principle of buying stock at a low price and selling them when they hit a conveniently high price, making a profit. This is not the only way to make profit in stock market, they can also use a short sell approach. With this approach, traders bet on prices collapse and It works this way: they borrow a stock, sell it and then buy it back to return it to the lender

There are certain requirements to start trading stocks:

1. You need a broker: Choosing the right broker that would be responsible for the security of your

funds, as they would be in charge of your investment, is essential. Having the right broker is key to how fast you can buy and sell stock. You would also need to have access to stocks from all around the world. The broker ensures that there is a large array of stock options for you to choose from. Having a broker makes it easy for you to choose the stocks that suit your swing trading needs.

2. You need a trading platform: This makes information about different stocks easily available. Information that would be useful for trades, from price history of the stocks to their current prices. These trading platforms gives a complete experience: they make possible for the traders to trade on their platforms giving access to different stocks around the world.

3. Decide you swing trading stock strategies: Trading strategies are used by traders to analyze

which direction the different stocks prices could take by using bits of information. This process is a priority. There are different strategies and different ways to run an analysis. The two main strategies that are usually considered all the time and are the parent of the other strategies are:

- Fundamental Analysis: This represents the study of specific information as well as basic information about the company whose stocks is being analyzed. You' ll need to know sales, debts, profit, products, new products launch, announcement, amongst many other information. This show the future of the company, the path its stock is likely to take, if the company is volatile or if the company is likely to make more profit.

- Technical Analysis: This is the identification of studied patterns about buying and selling that have led to swings in the past and have the ability to lead to more swings. These patterns are known by studying closely the price actions, historical patterns and different trading indicators.

- Price Action: This is basically the study of historical patterns in order to figure out the direction in which the stock prices or market would move next. It enables the trader to understand the action of the participants in the market (buyers and sellers) and the market itself. This helps the trader make good trading decisions. The candlesticks are the most commonly used price action indicator.

4. Channel Trading: This strategy depends on trends. It involves identifying stock with strong trends within a channel. Traders' actions usually depend on the trend, when the stock prices are in an uptrend you opt for buy options and vice versa.

5. Support Triggers: This is the basis for technical analysis. According to CMC "A support level indicates

a price level, or area on the chart, vbelow the current market price where buying is strong enough to overcome selling pressure. As a result, a decline in price is halted and price turns back up again. A stock swing trader would look to enter a buy trade on the bounce off the support line, placing a stop loss below the support line".

6. Resistance Triggers: This is the direct opposite of a support trigger. According to CMC "It represents a price level, or area, above the current market price where selling pressure may overcome buying pressure, causing the price to turn back down against an uptrend. In this case a swing trader could enter a sell position on the bounce off the resistance level, placing a stop loss above the resistance line. Remember when it comes to incorporating support and resistance into your swing trading system is that when price breaches a support or resistance level, they switch roles – what was once a support becomes a resistance, and vice versa."

ETF

Exchange traded funds (ETF) are commonly used by traders because it opens to many options, it is various. Traders are also keen on them because of the tight bid on spreads. It is easy for a beginner to trade ETFs because they are available in different levels and in different sectors. People can choose the industry, or sector, they are most skilled in and start trading. ETFs are a collection of multiple stocks called baskets; they are not prone to bullish movements as other single stocks but this also makes them less likely to move downwards too. This makes it less likely for traders to have capital losses, making it suitable for them to swing trade.

An important part of swing trading is being able to exit, or attain your position, when you want. This is important because of the short time frame and the constantly changing market status. Therefore, it is important that traders pick the right ETF.

What makes an ETF suitable? A fine swing trading environment, high volume and an increased activity in prices; these are acceptable and needed qualities of a right ETF, it allows traders to have an easy exit and entrance. The ability to exit and enter a trade is a part of swing trading that cannot be over emphasized. The very obvious downside of using a low volume ETF is being able to liquidate at a time of your choice. Simply put, exiting and entering isn't as easy.

After the process of finding good ETFs, the next and obvious step is to find a potential trade. Every trader knows that there is always a possibility of losing in a trade. There are technical forecasts, and trades can be based off of this forecast, even if no strategy, or forecast, can point out all the market price moves or predict correctly all the different ways the market can take. It is also important to use this tool to chart the course of your trade, at least to the point where it can be controlled. Traders use the available tools, charts patterns, to find moves that would most likely bring profit. Chart patterns are shapes on price charts of an ETF, they predict volatility in what direction it would increase and vice-versa.

OPTIONS

In swing trading, options (stock) are mostly used as a convenient replacement for underlying stock. Stock options are contract bounded by a short period of time, they give the "option buyer" the opportunity to either buy or sell a particular stock for a fixed price. The option grantor, or the seller, is giving the buyer an opportunity to buy stock at a fixed price.

There are peculiar terms to options trading, defining these terms are necessary to understand options. There are four major things to know:

- Option type: There are two types of options that can be bought or sold: call and put. The call is an option contract that allows you to buy stocks at a fixed price and at a particular time. The put is an option contract that allows you to sell stocks at a fixed price and at a particular time.

- The expiration date: it is when the time frame giving for the contract to be used relapses. At this point the contract becomes useless.

- Exercise price: this is also referred to as strike price. It is the price which the trader chooses to sell or buy the stock.

- Premium: This consists of intrinsic value and time value. It refers to the price paid for an option per share. The intrinsic value refers to the price of an option determined by price difference between the market price and the exercise price. While the Time value is the value of an option determined by the amount of time before the expiration date of the contract. This has a **major role in trades. The closer to the expiration date the more the price of the option drops.**

Unlike other instruments, terms like "up" and "down" can be used to describe how the trades are doing in the market, in options different terms are used:

- At the money: an option is said to be "at the money" when the exercise price is approximately equal to the stock price. That means that no one has an advantage, they are equal.

- In the money: this is when an option has intrinsic value: when the difference between the stock and Exercise prices is positive for the option trader. For the owner of the put option, when the price of the stock is lesser than the exercise price then the term "in the money" can be used. For another owner of a call option, when the price of the stock is greater than the Exercise price then "in the money" can be used.

- Out of the money: This is the complete opposite of the "in the money". This means there is less, or no profit at all, for the owner of the options.

For the owner of a call action the stock price is lesser than strike price, he can then be said to be out of money. For a put option owner, he is out of money when the stock price is greater than the exercise price.

Also, options has its own terms to describe option traders:

- The holders: these are the investors with the option contract, they own the contract. As usual they are divided into call holders and put holders. The call holders buy the stock adhering to the conditions in the contract. The put holder owns the right to sell the stock

- The writers: for beginners it is highly recommended to stay as holders till they master option strategies. Option writers sell the option contracts. They are given the premium by the holders and they, in exchange, promise to sell certain shares at the exercise priced. One of the reasons why beginners are encouraged to be holders is because risks is higher for the writer. The holders have little or no risk attached to owning the contract. They have the choice of doing nothing with the contracts, the only loss they may face is the money used to purchase the contract in the first place. The larger risk falls on the writer. It requires more option skills. The writer has an obligation to sell or buy at the exercise price and, sometime, they incorporate losses.

Swing Trading Options Strategies

As stated earlier, options swing trading has a high profit margin and many traders have moved to this 'world' just for this reason. As much as trading is risk centered it is also lucrative if done well. Options brings these profits with a level of security.

Choose the right stock: This is the first step in any market option. Many people's downturns start from making the wrong choice. Picking your stock may prove a difficult and confusing task, since there are several stocks to pick from. What to do, then? Have a watch list, monitor leading stocks and watch their moves, seek advice (if necessary), watch how the stocks are affected by external moves and then, start your options swing trading strategy.

- Know you Market: knowing your market will enhance successful trade. Knowing the strength and all the loopholes of your market would guide your choices as you go. It will help you decide if your trade should be for long periods or shorter periods. It is good to look out for bullish trends and know the volatility of the market. This would help you make other choices easily.

- Decide your exercise price: the next important step to make is you exercise, or strike, price. Your option strategies should help you with this decision. It is ideal to pick a price option that is "out of the money".

- Choose your expiration date: it is advisable to use monthly options; basically because your stock needs enough time to conveniently go through your exercise price in order to maximize the worth of your options. Trading strategies says: "As a general rule, if your expiration time is too big, on one hand, the risk decreases, but at the other one, the percentage gains decrease as well. In other words, if you' re buying more time, you' re going to get considerably less risk and your potential losses are going to be much smaller, as well as the profit."

- Maximize Exits and Entries: this is also important. It is ok to not have provided the best entries that can be dealt with, traders are patient enough.

FUTURES

A future is a contract to buy or sell a particular asset, or security, in the future and at a set time. The contracts are standard. The person who buys a future is taking the responsibility of buying and receiving the assets when the time stipulated on the contract elapses, at the same time, the seller of the contract is taking the responsibility of selling and delivering the underlying assets once the date on the contract expires.

According to "mytrading" skills:

"Speculators use futures contracts to speculate on the market and make a profit on falling or rising prices of the underlying instrument. Most futures contracts are not held until their execution date as they can be regularly traded through an exchange. The price of a futures contract depends on the current market price of the underlying instrument."

The future market is a place where traders can buy and sell future contracts. The commodities and assets traded aren't restricted to one thing, they go from crude oil to metals to beef and many other commodities.

Two important terms in futures trading are Hedging

and speculation. They are the two categories of traders in future trading and in other forms of trading. Though the hedgers and the Speculators are both traders in the future market they have different goals and purposes. "Hedging involves trading futures to keep intact the future prices of the commodity, or asset, taking delivery and selling the said commodity later in the cash market". This action protects future traders from the hassles of future price lists.

Speculation involves betting on the potential of price changes for profit.

For the future market, to be efficient, these two groups (Speculators and hedgers) must interact.

Steps to Trade Futures:

1. Knowledge: knowledge is key. Knowing as much as you can about futures is really important; understand the terms used, know what ventures are riskier than the others. Know the difference between the job of a speculator and a hedger.

2. Know the risk: knowing the risks involved and understanding them is also important. In trading futures, traders can have enormous gains and huge losses as well, depending on how well their trade does.

3. Managing your account: decide if you want to manage your account with the help of a broker or if you want to use an account run by professionals, trading companies or advisors.

4. Select a Broker: do your research; make sure the broker you pick has a license and is also a secured one. There are platforms that provide brokers and ensure the security of your assets and funds.

5. Learn about the platform: learn about your trading platform and its functionalities. Get comfortable using it. It is easier to trade futures, if you're confident with the platform. Become a professional.

6. Have a plan: every good future trader knows that a plan is essential. Winging it would not cut it in trading. You need a trading plan for everything you do. Having a plan prepares you and makes it easy for you to track your performances.

7. Pick your contract: as difficult as this might be, having help and asking the right questions in relation to your commodities and assets would help you a lot.

There are several future strategies:

1. Trend-following: this is one of the most used strategies, even outside future. It has been tested and considered effective and not as tasking as many other strategies. This strategy is simply moving in the direction of a trend (underlying). Simply put, if the trend moves up, the trader following the trend would look for long positions, if the trend moves down the trader looks for short positions. We all know that in an uptrend

and downtrend there are higher highs and higher lows, lower highs and lower lows respectively. The best time to buy when there is an uptrend is noticed to be at the higher low. The same goes for the downtrends, you have to pick the lower highs though.

2. Fundamental trading strategies: as technical as many of these future strategies are, it is important to note that the fundamentals play a major role in the trends and in the support and resistance of strategies. So, knowing the current development on the fundamentals of the instruments used, is important for traders. A large part of the decisions made by fundamental traders is based more on Fundamentals than the technical aspect of trading. The problems with fundamentals are usually solved with the technical aspect of trading. For example, fundamentals usually determine whether to look for long or short positions, the technicals are to use for price

levels. Following fundamental releases is also important. This shows we're the economy is heading and the possible outcomes of futures.

3. The Pullback: a Pullback is a pause in an asset or security's trend. The term is mainly used in association with the price drops that happen in a short period of time. In an uptrend the prices usually break above the standard resistance level, during the downtrends the prices usually break below a standard support level. Pullbacks usually maximize a part of technical analysis: "*When an important support or resistance level breaks, that level changes its nature and becomes a resistance or support level, respectively*". "*A broken support level becomes a resistance level, and a broken resistance level becomes a support level. This is especially true on higher timeframes, such as the daily, although it can also be observed on shorter-term timeframes, such as*

the 30-minutes or 1-hour ones.". This is according to my tradingskills.com

4. Counter-trend: This strategy is how its name goes: it counters trend. Basically, it goes in the opposite direction of the underlying trend. This is a risky strategy, even in comparison to other risky strategies. Like every other risky strategy, counter trend should be done by traders with experience. An example of how Counter-trend works is basically the opposite of trend-following, traders during an uptrend sell and during a downtrend buy.

There are several other strategies to be used in trading futures. Some of these are peculiar to futures while other are not. There are also strategies that are used for other forms of trading that shouldn't be applied in futures. A few of the strategies to avoid are:

1. Scalping: As popular as it is, it requires a high level of skill and professionalism. People tend to

confuse short-term as simple and run into it. Scalping has produced a large number of losses for many different traders. It is exciting and attractive, especially to new traders though. To get profit regularly while scalping experience is the key. Swing trading futures is a safer strategy than Scalping and even more for new traders.

2. Illiquid trading: liquidity attracts a large number of buyers and sellers at different price levels. Illiquid are in state and can fluctuate a lot, this leads to major losses.

CRYPTOCURRENCY

Cryptocurrency swing trading involves trading your altcoins by holding position for a couple of weeks or months. A lot of traders nowadays switched to swing trade cryptocurrency. Day traders in order to increase their profit tend to increase the volume of trades, though this doesn't necessarily equate the expected large profit. The increase volume may also lead to increased losses too. With cryptocurrency it is important for the traders to watch the market, if they are going to continuously make decisions that are important for their trade. Here are a few terminologies a trader should be familiar with in swing trading cryptocurrency.

1. Altcoin: This is used to refer to any form of cryptocurrency that isn't bitcoin; it is basically an alternative to it. There are several altcoins: Manero, dash, ripple, zcash, Litecoin etc..

2. ATH: This is an acronym for all-time high. Professional traders know that this might not be one of the greatest times to buy a coin.

3. ATL: This is all time low. It refers to the lowest price an asset has ever been at.

4. CMP: Current market price

5. HODL: This means that a trader was in possession of the coin till the desired price was reached. It is also "Hold" misspelled.

6. Trading signals: This are meant to be a trader's guide to making trading decisions.

7. Wallet: This is a digital bank for the trader's assets.

8. Whales: As it is generally in the business world, they refer to big institutions or individuals with enough power to control the movement of prices.

9. Bag holder: This is used to describe a person who held on to an asset for a long time till it began to decrease in value to the point that it becomes worthless in the market

10. Block chain: This is a record of all the transactions that ever occurred, from the very first (genesis) to the current transaction. It is called 'historical record'.

11. Breaking: This is a drop-in price.

Cryptocurrencies swing trading has gained

popularity in the past few years. With more people venturing into it, it is best cryptocurrency practices are learnt to ensure successful trades:

1. Stop loss: Do not start a trade without the stop loss option. This allows you to cut your losses on time. This step gives you control, you can decide how much loss hits you during a trade. Professional traders always include this option in their trade.

2. Price change: it is important to monitor price changes on your coins. If you notice an increment in the prizes of your coins, usually about 20% whilst other coins are moving in the opposite direction, it is important that you consider to sell. When this happens more than 60% of the times the coins always drop to about half the price the next days. Do not get carried away or get greedy, walk out with the profit when you can.

3. Announcements: This is usually a warning to traders; smart ones know that you close your position before

the announcement. If an announcement is supposed to be made the next day, it might be something that may have a significant effect on your coins and your transactions. Close your position.

Add the above three to your other strategies and you should be counting more wins than heavy losses.

Advantages:

- Easy use: it isn't as complicated as it seems. It is easy to use and execute. Trading platforms and helps, made it easier. You can trade faster and handle more than one trade at a time, once you' ve learned. Though, the fact that it is easy doesn't mean you have to learn everything at once. Take your time to perfect the trade, learn the basics and the somewhat complicated parts before fully diving in. Using Demos helps a lot in your learning process.

- Closely linked to trading stocks: some of the useful skills used in trading stocks can also apply to swing trading cryptocurrency. Many stockbrokers with spare money venture into crypto swing trading. The difference between the two is the time frame.

- Several options to choose from: normally, in stock swing trading, there is the tendencie to be a drag because of the length of time it takes to finish a trade. With cryptocurrency this isn't an issue; a trader doesn't have to wait days to close a position. New positions can be opened before the old ones are closed. In this case you can trade and make gains from different altcoins in the space of minutes.

- Pattern day trading rule: according to Bulls on Wall street

"The pattern day trader rule is a law that prohibits individuals with US brokers with less than $25,000 from making more than three days trades per week

However, there is no pattern day trading rule in

cryptocurrencies. You can open a $200 account if you wanted to with a cryptocurrency exchange and buy and sell as many cryptocurrencies as you want every day. This means that if you do have a strategy with an edge trading cryptocurrency, you have the potential to grow a small account much faster than trading a small stock account with a US broker.".

Disadvantages:

As advantageous as swing trading cryptocurrency is, it also has a couple of disadvantages. Money will be lost, whether you accept it or not. So, learn not to trade on high margins. Take calculated risks and use swing trade practices to cushion your losses. Other possible disadvantages of swing trading cryptocurrencies are:

- Taxes: swing trading doesn't stop you from paying your taxes. Your taxes are supposed to be paid at the end of every trade profit, or not especially if you defaulted in the previous payments. This becomes a problem if you let them pile up.

- Time factor: You have to monitor the market movement as regularly as every hour and be prepared to act accordingly. Leaving the market unmonitored, is a risky venture. It can be a little stress for those with full time jobs.

CHAPTER 6
TOOLS AND PLATFORMS FOR SWING TRADING

A trading platform is an electronic software that allows a trader to be able to open, close and manage market positions through a broker.

Most brokers offer online trading platforms either free or on the condition that the account has to be funded consistently and should be able to make a specified number of trades per month. Trading platforms are usually targeted to a specific market such stocks, currency market, foreign exchange (forex), and more.

How to pick the best trading platform

There are hundreds of attractive trading platforms out there so, it's up to you how you get to choose the best trading platform that suits your market.

The fees and features depend on your market, most traders may prefer to go for trading platforms with lower fees, but the disadvantage of it is that it may probably have lower features and less information research.

Some traders, mostly short-term traders, might prefer platforms with level 2 quotes and market depth charts; 'level 2 quotes' is a service that is based on a subscription that gives you a free access to NASDAQ order book. Option traders might prefer tools that are made to see options techniques and strategies.

Pick the platform that has unique features that are in line with your preference and market. It's not all about the cost or fee associated with it, choose the one that fits you best.

Trading tools and platforms

- Interactive brokers:

This is the most popular platform for most professional traders, it usually has relatively lower fees and access to various kinds of markets.

- TDAmeritade:

This is a platform for both traders and investors

- Robinhood:

This trading platform began as a mobile app, but has now progressed into a web interface, it is a trading platform that has no commission attached to it. It is usually targeted at millennials. The advantage of this platform is that it can get you cash from various sources, ranging from interest on cash in accounts and selling order flow to bigger brokerages.

- MetaTrader:

This platform is one of the most popular platforms for forex traders. The MQL scripting embedded in it, is usually used to automate trading in currencies.

- TradeStation:

This platform is usually targeted at algorithmic traders that usually implement and execute strategies using automated scripts built with *EasyLanguage*.

- MetaStock:

This platform offers over 300 built-in drawing tools for technical indicators. Fibonacci retracement is a typical drawing tool that uses complement technical indicators, and fundamental data with screening and filtering criteria.

- Worden TC2000:

This platform provides the solution for U.S and Canadian stocks and funds. Some credible features of this platform include instant messaging, news, sorting, scanning, alerts and watchlists. It also contains 10 drawing tools and over 70 technical indicators with a user interface very easy to use. The cons of this platform are that it offers automated trading tools and asset classes are limited to stocks, funds, and ETFs. The pro of this platform is that it has a backtesting function based on historical data.

- eSignal:

This platform offers research capabilities. It has a vast coverage across multiple assets classes such as stocks, funds, bonds, derivatives and forex. The features of this platform depend on the package you are working with. eSignal is very good with trade management interface accompanied with news and fundamental figures coverage, and its stock charts software allows you to customize it to your preference. However, Backtesting, alert and some technical indicators tends to be lacking in this platform.

- NinjaTrader:

This is another trading software that provides you with an end to end solution from an order entry to execution. It also provides customized option with a third-party library integration that is very compatible for more than 100 apps and add-on products. It is targeted to futures and forex traders.

The NinjaTrader also contains useful trade simulators, 100+ technical indicators, fundamental charting and research tools. It provides these tools in order to give risk free environment to work with. This software is free to use for backtesting, advanced charting and trade simulation. A free version of this platform is available for live trading once a user pays his license fee.

- INO MarketClub:

This provides the solution for users that are looking for a charting software with technical indicators, trend lines, quantitative analysis tools and filtering functionality that is integrated with a charting and trading system. This trading software is targeted to forex, ETFs and precious metals.

- Automated Trading Software:

This software analyzes security price charts and other multiple time frames. It identifies technical signals which includes; recognition of patterns, spread discrepancies, price trends, and news that impacts the market. for instance, if a software that uses criteria the user sets identifies a currency pair trade that satisfies the predetermined parameters for profitability

- Wave59 PRO2:

This platform provides a high-end functionality for the trader, including hive technology artificial intelligence module, market astrophysics, and pattern building and matching. It also offers advanced level products.

- EquityFeed Workstation:

One unique feature of this software is a stock hunting tool called "FilterBuilder" it is built on a numerous number of filtering criteria that helps traders to assess and chose stocks with each of their desired parameter. Some other experts say that it has the best stock screening software around level 2.

This software or platform also contains numerous market data which includes both OTC and PinkSheet markets. Although it offers some limited technical indicators and no backtesting or automated trading.

- Profit Source:

the unique features of this platforms include Elliot wave analysis and backtesting functionality and over 30+ automated technical indicators developed in its asset class coverage spans across equities, forex, options, futures and funds at the global level. This trading software is usually targeted at short term traders with entry and exit strategies.

- VectorVest:

VectorVest covers more geographical region than any other trading platform that is available today. It contains comprehensive technical indicators across major stocks around the world today. It also has unique features of back testing functions, customizability functions, real-time filtering, charting tools and watch lists.

CHAPTER 7
FUNDAMENTAL ANALYSIS

Fundamental analysis is a way of measuring a security's value by checking out some basic factors such as economic and financial related factors. The ultimate goal of every financial analyst is to check every possible thing that can alter a security's intrinsic value. Ranging from industrial factors to macroeconomic factors passing through microeconomic factors as a measure of the effectiveness of a company's management.

The goal of the fundamental analyst is to reach a certain number that he or investor can use to compare with the current price of a security, so that they can find out if a particular security is devalued or overvalued. Fundamental analysis is quite different from technical analysis because it checks out movement of price of a security while the fundamental analysis talks about the change in value of a security.

Fundamental analysis is usually done from a bigger to smaller perspective so that the stocks or security that are not well priced can be identified. Fundamental analysts carefully study through the whole economy state and the strength of a particular industry, then they concentrate on how the performance of the company, so that lately they can finally know the average market value of a stock.

This type of analysis uses public data to check out a stock' s or security' s value. For instance, suppose an analyst wants to perform a fundamental analysis on the value of a bond. He can probably carry out the analysis by checking out interest rates and the economy state, or by carrying out a research on bond issuer and potential changes in credit rating. Fundamental analysts also utilize revenue, earnings, future growth, return on equity, profit margins and some other data to check out a company' s value and possibilities for a future growth. Those information can be found in the financial statement of a company.

Investments and fundamental analysis

The work of a fundamental analyst is to be able to develop a good model that traders can use to measure the value of a company's share price based on the data that was obtained publicly. The analyst should be able to give his own opinion about if the company's share price should worth. As compared to recent market price. Most analysts might just simply refer to their own measured price as the company's intrinsic value.

Most of the time, investors publish a buy (a buy refers to the process of acquiring a possession or goods or service for a payment) when they calculate their stocks value higher than the stock's current market price. Such analysts should be able to purchase stocks with recommendations that are favourable because those stocks might have some probability of rising with time.

On the other hand, stocks with prices that are not favourable have a very high probability of falling over time. Fundamental analysis are classified under two major categories:

- Quantitative analysis
- Qualitative analysis

QUANTITATIVE FUNDAMENTAL ANALYSIS

Quantitative analysis here refers to measurable attribute of something, they are numbers that are measurable. They can be gotten from financial statements, profits, assets and can be measured with great precision.

- Financial statements:

Financial statements are ways by which a company passes on an information concerning their financial performance and progress levels. Smart fundamental analysts use quantitative information to make their investments decisions. Financial statements are:

Income statements

Balance sheets

Cash flow statements

- BALANCE SHEETS

This involves all company's assets, liabilities and equity at a specific period of time. The equation for the balance sheet is stated below:

ASSETS = LIABILITIES + EQUITY OF SHAREHOLDER

Liabilities and shareholder's equity refers to how the company acquire their assets, while the asset refers to what the company own such as cash etc.

- INCOME STATEMENT

The role of the income statement is to show a company's revenues and expenses information over a given time frame.

- CASH FLOW STATEMENT

Cash flow statement refers everything related to the way cash comes into and goes out of the company.

QUALITATIVE FUNDAMENTAL ANALYSIS

This refers to the quality of a company, its staff and executives, brand, brand name recognition and patents. There are some essential attributes that every qualitative fundamental has to look at critically.

- Business model:

They have to pay close attention to the business model of a company

- Competitive advantage:

The rewards that most shareholder enjoy when they maintain competitive advantage is insatiable. The success of a company depends on their ability to be competitively advantaged.

- Management:

Another cause of the success of most businesses today, most of them are still around today because of good managers and planners.

- Corporate Governance:

This refers to the policies and laws made within an institution that shows the various relationships between stake holders, directors and management. These laws are defined and instituted by the company. They have a way of affecting things in the business.

In qualitative analysis, it is also very important to consider: industry growth, company' s competition, business cycles, company base, and industry and market share among various firms. An investor can only understand the financial status and progress only when he has learnt about how a company' s industry works.

CHAPTER 8
TECHNICAL ANALYSIS

This is a swing trading aspect that is used to check out investments and find out opportunities for trading by analyzing statistical trends, such as price movement and volume. The ultimate goal of a technical analyst is to evaluate a stock' s or security' s value. Technical analysis tools are usually used to check out the various ways the supply or demand of a specific security can affect the security' s change in price, volume and implied volatility. Even though that it may be used to source short term trading signals from a lot of charting tools, it can also evaluate the strength of a security that is relative to a broader market.

Technical trading applies to any stock or security with a common historical data, such as stocks, currencies, futures, commodities and other securities. Technical analysis is usually used more in commodities and forex markets than any other market. That's exactly where trader focus on short-term price movements.

Technical analysis defined

Technical analysis works on an assumption that a past trading activity and changes in price of a specific security are clear indicators of the security's movements in price compared with accurate investing and trading rules. Normal retail traders might make their decisions based on price charts of a stock, or security, but professional analysts make use of technical analysis with other forms of research before make crucial decisions based on their trade.

One of the greatest supports to technical analysts around the world, is the collection of chartered analysts. The designation of the chartered market technician can be gotten after three exams that have technical analysis tools.

General assumptions for technical analysis

The two major ways of analyzing and evaluating securities are: fundamental analysis and technical analysis, refer to the previous chapter to know more about fundamental as it was exhaustively explained. There are some assumptions that have been used for technical analysis:

Firstly, markets are very efficient with values representing factors that influences a securities price.

Secondly, random markets moving trends and patterns that are identifiable usually tends to repeat itself with time.

Other assumptions include:

- The market discounts everything

Can you believe that most technical analysts think that everything ranging from a company's fundamentals to every market factor out there are already priced? This perspective matches with the efficient market hypothesis. This is a hypothesis that says that share price will show all possible information and consists of alpha generation. In the EMH, security will always trade at their fair value on exchanges. This makes it difficult for investors and analysts to buy devalued securities and sell for some inflated prices.

Moreover, it is very difficult to outperform the whole market expert and market timing.

- Price moves in trends

Most professional technical analysts expect that prices will show some trends despite the time frame accompanied with some market movements. Many analysts base on this assumption.

- History tends to repeat itself

Technical analysts see the movements in price associated with market psychology. This tends to be quite true; price movements are predictable based on emotions such as excitement and fear. Technical analysis uses patterns in charts to evaluate these emotions and progressive movements in markets in order to understand trends. Despite the fact that many have been used for over a millennium today, they still seem to be essential because they are able to show patterns in price movements.

The repetitive nature of price movements is usually associated with market psychology.

How can I apply technical analysis to my trade?

Technical analysis is used to foretell any possible movements in price of any stock or security that is tradable, and that follow the rules of supply and demand such as currency, currency pairs, stocks, bonds, forex and futures. Most persons even think at technical analysis as the study of the supply and demand when they are seen in price movements of a stock. Even though that technical applies to price changes most analysts use it to check other numbers such as trading volumes.

Here, I will be showing you some professional patterns and signals that have been built to support technical analysts today. There are hundreds, if not thousands, of patterns and signals that have been developed to aid technical analysis. Some have built various kind of trading systems that will aid them to be able to foretell and identify price movements. In fact, some of these indicators are targeted at seeking the current market trend which includes support and resistance regions. While others are focused on checking out the strength and continuation of a trend. Here are some of the visual indicators that technical analyst use.

Moving averages

Oscillators

Support and resistance levels

Volume and momentum indicators

Price trends

Chart patterns

Some limitations to technical analysis

One major criticism to technical analysis is that history doesn't always repeat itself, so price pattern study is of no importance and can obviously be ignored.

Another criticism is that it works only in few cases. For instance, most technical traders usually place stop-loss order below 200 day moving average of a company. If most traders have done so, and security gets to that price, there will be a large number of sales. That can push the stock down.

Other traders will then see the price reducing and also sell their positions. Strengthening the trend.

Major differences between technical and fundamental analysis

Fundamental analysts' focuses on evaluating and measuring the value of securities, they get to research and study everything from overall economy to the financial conditions.

Technical analysis is quite different from fundamental analysis because it measures the price changes and volume as the only inputs. They don't measure a security's value, they identify patterns and trends that can show what a security will look like in future.

CHAPTER 9
RISK MANAGEMENT

Since the goal of every good trader is to make profit, to be a good and successful one you have to learn how to manage risks associated with your trading and how to protect your profits. How well you manage your risks determines how successful you will be as a trader.

Prepare your mind because you are about to learn very simple but powerful and practical techniques in risk management strategies and techniques.

PLANNING YOUR TRADE

A Chinese military general, Sun Tzu once said: "Every battle is won before it is fought", this implies that planning and strategy is very important in trading. Planning is inevitable. It is just like the popular quote says "Plan the trade and trade the plan". This determines the success or failure of your trade, no successful trader goes into trade without carefully planning out the trade, pointing out possible future losses, calculating risks and listing out possible future profits in your trade.

A plan should be written down clearly and concisely, your plan can change with changes in market, risks tolerance should also be incorporated. Here are some steps you must follow for a successful trade plan:

- Skill Assessment: here you should be able to assess yourself very well to determine how ready you are to trade. You should ask yourself very crucial question such as: are you ready to trade? How much confidence do you have in a particular market? Have you tested your system by *paper trading*? (paper trading is a way of practicing buying and selling without investing real money, it is usually done using online trading platforms such as *paperMoney* and *Investopedia*) How sure are you that your system will work in a live trading environment? Can you spot and follow your signals without delaying?

- Mental preparation: As a good trader you should emotionally and mentally prepared for the upcoming tasks, you should be prepared for whatever situation that might arise and whatever changes that may occur in your market. Avoid distractions as much as possible in your trading area. If you are emotionally incapable, try taking a day off, take some rest, do some exercise. This keeps your brain ready for the upcoming task because trading has a lot of thinking associated with it.

Also have a market mantra before the day begin, it is a kind of special quote or phrase that gets you ready for trading.

- Set Risk Level: this determines how much of your portfolio you should risk on a trade. Your portfolio includes all financial assets, such as bonds, stocks, and currencies, cash, commodities and cash equivalents. This depends on how you choose to trade and the risks tolerance; It can vary, but it should be within the range of 1% to 5% of your portfolio on a given trading day. If you lose any of that amount of money in a day, leave that market immediately and save your portfolio for a better market.

CONSIDER THE ONE-PERCENT RULE

Most successful traders make use of what is called the one-percent rule; it simply states that you should never invest more than 1% of your capital or portfolio into a single trade or market. This means that if you have $10,000 in your trading account, the highest amount you would invest should not be above $100 per single trade.

This technique is usually done by traders with account with less than $100,000. Some other traders may decide to go as high as 2%. It all depends on your position and the size of your account. The best thing to do is to keep the rule at least below 2%.

SETTING STOP-LOSS AND PROFIT POINTS

Just like the name implies, a stop-loss point occurs when a trader decides to sell a stock and bear the loss, this situation usually happens when the market doesn' t turn out well enough for the trader. The stock' s in the market goes way below expected, hence before the stock' s value could get any lower the trader decides to sell it out.

The take profit point is the price at which a trader will sell a stock and gain a profit from the trade. Traders usually sell before a period of consolidation takes place.

HOW TO MORE EFFECTIVELY SET STOP-LOSS POINTS

Setting stop-loss points in order to have profit is normally done in technical analysis, although fundamental analysis can help out.

A great way of setting stop-loss or take profit levels

is by resistance trend lines; this can be done by connecting and comparing previous highs or lows.

DIVERSIFY AND HEDGE

To diversify and hedge is just like the popular phrase "never put all your eggs in one basket" . If you decide to put all your money in one stock you are taking a big risk. So spread your investments across different sectors. There may also be times when you need to hedge at a particular position considering a stock and the market.

THE BOTTOM LINE

As a good trader you should be able to know when to enter or leave a trade. By using the stop-loss, the trader can minimize losses. It is better to plan ahead of time.

CALCULATING EXPECTED RETURN

Calculating expected returns is very crucial in managing risks, it helps you think through your trade and it is a very good way to compare trades in order to choose the most profitable and less risky ones. Returns can be calculated thus:

[(Probability of gain) × (take profit % gain)] + [(probability of loss) × (stop-loss % loss)]

The result of this calculation will give you your expected returns.

TRADING RISKS

To become a successful trader, you need to aware of the various risks that you are bound to face before getting into the trading world. There are three major categories of risks:

Market risks

Understanding market changes in your trade is a very important aspect of your trade. Understanding when the markets rises and falls coupled with the possible risks associated with it will help you to protect more your profit. Types of market risks include:

- Inflation risk: inflation occurs when there is an uncertainty in the future value of an investment you are making. While a deflation may mean more returns and profit for you. A rising inflation often reduces the returns and profit you'd be expecting from it. This also means that as prices of stocks and commodities increases, the demand for it reduces. Hence, you should prepare your plan for any market changes at all.

- Marketability risk: this tells how sellable your investment is. If there is any form of resistance or delay in selling or marketing your investment effectively, then your target market won't mean anything. For example, if you choose to invest in a small company whose stock isn't sold on one of the major stock markets, then you risk losing your investment for nothing.

- Currency translation risk: this usually occurs when you are trading with foreign countries, when there are fluctuations between the values of your local currency and the currency of your trading foreign country. A good knowledge about currency trading risk would be very beneficial to traders because even if your stock or investment rises in price you can still lose money based on the currency exchange rate between the two countries. If the value of your local currency falls against the other currency, your investment can be far smaller when you convert it back.

INVESTMENT RISKS

This suggests how you invest your money and manage how you enter into or leave trades. There are two major types of risks:

- Opportunity risks: this type of investment risk shuts, or stops, you from investing in other more profitable trades due to the fact that your money is already tied up in your current trade. This type of risk makes you lose golden opportunities, all because your money is blocked by another one.

- Concentration risks: this happens when you focus all your investment and capital in just one particular trade, perhaps because you think that you have found your dream trade that will make you a millionaire. Hence you invest all you've got, leaving yourself very vulnerable to any potential risks that might arise in that trade with the possibility of losing it all.

TRADING RISKS

Trading risks are common risks that swing traders usually encounters and every trader needs to know about them; just as the saying "knowledge *is power*", you need to be knowledgeable about them, and this will give you a leverage in managing future risks that may arise. Some common risks that are associated with trading risks includes:

- Slippage risk: this risk focuses on some hidden costs that may be associated with every transaction the trader makes. Every time you enter or leave a trade there are some very minor and little subtraction of money from your account. Also, every time you buy a stock at the ask price, which is the lowest price available for the stock that you want, and sell it at the bid price which is highest price someone is willing to pay for your shares, you have to know that it is always less than the ask price. At first, the amount for each trade may seem small but as your trading increases, the amounts you lose also increases.

- Poor execution risk: this risk occurs when your broker has a difficult time in filling out your order, perhaps due to fast market conditions, poor availability of stock and the absence of other buyers and sellers. When this happens, you risk have your stock trade going below than it should or not getting your order filled at all.

- Gap risk: this occurs when there are price gaps in your transactions; sometimes a stock opens at a significantly high or lesser price and sometimes may trade through your exit price. For example, a stock may close at $25 today and open at $20 tomorrow. If your planned price is $24 your order is likely to be filled out at the opening price. Although these types of risk are rare, it can cause problems for most traders.

OTHER TYPES OF RISKS INCLUDE:

BLACK SWAN EVENTS: these are the type of risks that comes up unexpectedly. They are very hard to predict. It is a type of large risk that has great impact on the market.

SOVEREIGN RISKS: when a sovereign risk occurs, the bond market falls with yields skyrocketing while at the same time depreciating the country' s currency value. Causing breaks in trading and more losses to abound. A typical example of this kind of risk includes Argentina and Mexico which delayed on paying back their loans back in the 1970' s pushing their respective currencies to record lows.

UNDIVERSIFIED RISK: this is a type of risk that occurs when you *'put all your eggs in one basket'*. This type of risk is usually very hard to avoid and difficult to predict as markets can also influence this type of risk. This type is one of the major reasons why investors and traders usually decides to diversify their stocks and money, avoiding the risk of losing everything at once.

CAUSES OF LOSSES

As a good trader you need to be in control of everything you do and everything that happens in your market. You are already on your way to becoming a successful trader, if you are able to eliminate great losses that might arise. Here, I am going to be mentioning some causes of big losses in your trade:

Stubbornness: this happens when we find it very difficult to admit our mistakes. This is the main reason most traders suffer losses in their trades. It doesn't matter how much you know, if you cannot learn to follow price action more than your own ideas, it can really cost you a lot. Give yourself a break when you find yourself in making great losses.

Oversizing: putting too much into a trade is also one of the causes of losses most traders face today. When you put too much in just one trade, quitting it may be a very difficult thing to do. Because it means you have to risk having all those moneys leave your account.

Don't trade sizes that makes you uncomfortable. Trade sizes that you can easily afford and won't matter much if you lose it. Imagine when you have $50,000 in your account and lose $300 in a trade, it will barely affect your net worth right? Even if you lose it on consistent basis, it will still barely affect your net worth. But then imagine when you have that same $50,000 in your account and lose out $2000 on a trade, that's a big loss for a single trade right? On the first example you might not really see it as a loss, but as time goes trust me you will begin to see the visible losses from it, that is exactly what happens when you invest too much in particular trade, when there are losses you are the first person to suffer from them. The bigger you trade the more you are vulnerable to potential losses in that trade.

Being in a losing position: if you are on the wrong side of a trade you are risking a lot, most traders think that they have finally reached their dream trade, that will make them millionaires, but they don't know that they are on the wrong side of the trade. By the time they realize it, they have already started making huge losses already. Always make sure that you are in a winning position, check statistics, check records find out the trends, and find out the best. Assess yourself and make sure that you are not in a bad trade or position.

No trading plan: this was part of what we talked about in risk management techniques, just like the popular quote says *"he who fails to plan, plans to fail"*, planning and preparation is inevitable if you really want to become a successful trader. Lack of good preparation is one of the major causes of huge losses today. How do you start a trade without setting goals, assessing your skills, setting risk tolerance levels, checking risk/reward ratios?

The reason you suffer big losses when you don't plan very well is because there is no exit strategy for you when the market goes bad. Most traders think that when you purchase a new stock, it will start profiting immediately and everything will go as planned, but it doesn't work like this. You have to prepare yourself for any possible risk that your market may bring to you.

This means that your trade plan should flexible enough to accommodate to changes in various market conditions, whether the market goes in your favour or not. You have already planned out your entry and exit strategies. You have to be well prepared for the worst to happen for each trade you enter into.

No trading system: every good and successful trader

has a proven and quantified price action trading system. If yours is just any random trading system, then you should be ready to suffer from regular losses.

Trading systems such as automated trading, algorithmic trading (algorithmic trading is a of carrying out orders using automated and pre-programmed trading instructions to account for variables such as price, volume and timing. An algorithm is a set of directions for solving a problem), and mechanical trading, are trading systems that traders use to establish specific rules for both trade entries and exits. Once they are programmed, they can be executed in a computer. Traders make use of this method to execute and monitor their trades.

Automated trading systems usually requires the use of a software that is linked to a direct access broker example of such includes *TradeStation, NinjaTrader*.

Most traders make use of automated trading systems since they minimize errors as much as possible but they are also the reason why most traders suffer major losses.

Too much hope for a reversal: this happens when you are thinking that your market can go against your favour and must always return to current price levels.

Bad position sizing parameters: most traders suffer major setback and losses when they put their trade in a very bad position. Their market and trade are not based on historical evidences, statistics and worst-case scenarios.

Lack of discipline: some traders are just too lazy to create good trading systems for their trades, monitor environmental, currency and market changes and that is exactly why they suffer huge setbacks and losses. For most of them, even if they have a good trading system, it so hard to follow it.

Other causes of losses are:

Selling short in an uptrend

Buying in a downtrend

Too much ego to take a loss

WHEN TO STOP LOSS

No one wants to lose out money on a particular trade due to market price fluctuations and this is exactly where stop loss orders comes into play. Stop loss orders helps you limit large losses due to price fluctuations within the market. In order to set stop loss orders in your trade, there are three basic things you have to take into consideration. Those are:

- What is a stop-loss order?
- When is it convenient to set a stop-loss order?
- Where to set a stop-loss order?

I. What is a stop-loss order?

A stop-loss order is an order that you place with your broker to buy or sell a certain stock of yours when it gets to a certain price in order to limit and minimise your losses as much as possible. Without a stop-loss there is a risk of having huge losses on any transaction you make. Traders that work without stop-losses are at a slippage price risk. Refer to trade risks to know more about slippage price risk. But for explanation sake, slippage price risks are the ones that incurred when buying and selling stocks takes place, it happen when you are not able to find buyers for your stock at a certain price, causing you to sell the stock at a lower than expected. To become a successful trader you need to learn to place stop-losses; this way, you can have an idea of how much you can lose from a trade.

Setting stop-losses also helps to determine *position size* which we will be explaining extensively in the next chapter. If you don't set a stop-loss, it won't be very easy to select a position size that aligns with the account size.

Now, I will be using an illustration to explain a point here. Suppose you decided to purchase a stock at $70. Then immediately after purchasing the stock, you contact your broker and place an order with a stop-loss at $68. This means that when the price of that stock gets to $68 or below this value, the stock should be sold out immediately to avoid further losses. The risk involved in this scenario shouldn't be above 1%. Now, you can see how stop-loss is designed in order to minimise losses in trades as much as possible. The good thing about stop losses is that it costs nothing to implement it. The regular commission that you give your broker is the same while implementing stop-losses. Another good thing about stop-losses is that it helps you eliminate emotional influences from when making decisions in trading. The best thing to do is to be sure about your strategy and execute your plan. Stop-loss orders can help you stay on track.

ii. When to place stop-loss orders:

The ideal moment to set your stop-loss orders should be when writing out your trade plan, which is before you even start trading. More precisely, after setting out your goals. Your stop-loss should be clearly stated there so that you won't have any more future losses. However, some other traders might decide to set the stop-loss order later on, as they get to know more about their trade. With the knowledge you will acquire from this book, you should be able to set your stop-loss as quick as possible.

iii. Where to set your stop-loss orders:

Determining where to set your stop-loss is all about incorporating an allowable risk to your pricing. More in detail, it is about giving your stock price a threshold for buying or selling that stock. The pricing should be done with the intention of limiting losses as much as possible. It is very important to know where to set your stop-loss before you start trading.

Your stop-loss should be placed very close to your entry price, bear in mind that if it is too far apart it can cause you huge losses. For example, suppose you buy a stock at $25 your stop-loss should be within the range of $23-$24, it shouldn't be too far apart, otherwise you'd be losing out a lot.

FIXED STOP-LOSS METHOD:

Some other traders make use of a fixed stop-loss method, this happens when you have a fixed stop-loss amount. It may vary slightly based on the time frame or market conditions, but it should get too far apart from the fixed amount. Figuring out where to place your stop-loss highly depends on your risk threshold. For instance, a trader can set his fixed stop-loss to nothing less than $2, regardless of any market fluctuations. Your risk loss shouldn't go below that threshold.

PERCENTAGE STOP-LOSS METHOD:

Percentage stop-loss method guards or secure your losses at a specific percentage. For example, if you buy a stock for $23 per share. You can set a stop-loss order for $20.50. This will guard your loss to 10%. But in case the stock's price drops below $22.50, your shares will be sold at the current price. This method is used by most traders.

SUPPORT METHOD:

In this method, the investor or trader makes his research and determines the latest support level of the stock and places the stop-loss just below that level. The support method involves making hard stops at a set price.

In the support method the trader or investors focus is mainly on stock and the fixed prices that other traders use on that stock. At the first instance this method may look complicated to practice but it will look more realistic as time goes on.

MOVING AVERAGE METHOD:

Understanding the moving average method can really take you far as a trader. In the moving average method, the trader places the stop-loss just below a longer term moving average price rather than just short term prices.

The moving average price is a price that is calculated by analysing data points and creating a series of averages of different subset of the full data set. This method is usually used for technical analysis. In this method, the moving average price is usually calculated to help smooth out the price data by creating a constantly updated average price. This method minimises short term fluctuations.

POSITION SIZING

Position sizing in swing trading is the number of unit/shares that an investor or trader should invest in a trade in order to minimise risks and maximise returns. It is the size of position or the amount of money that an investor is going to trade. Investors use position sizing to determine the amount of units they can use to invest in a specific trade. When an investor is determining position sizing, he also has to consider his account size and risk tolerance. His account size is the total amount of money he has in his account for investing while his risk tolerance can be defined by his total allowable risk. In fact, investors that are able to calculate their risk tolerance can design a portfolio that benefits their tolerance in the long term.

Now, before an investor can properly determine his position size, he has to consider three major factors. Those are:

1. Account risk:

The first thing that an investor has to consider when determining his accurate position size is to check his account risk, which is usually expressed as a percentage of the investor's capital. Most fund traders don't usually risk more than 2% of their capital on a particular trade. While most traders don't risk more 2% of their capital on a trade. That 2% is their account risk. This type of account risk is called the *2% rule,* which we will be taking a deeper look in the next section.

THE 2% RULE: this is a rule investors use while investing in a particular trade and is implemented when an investor chooses not to risk more than 2% of their available capital on a particular trade. In order to execute and implement the 2% rule, the investor firstly needs to calculate what 2% of their available trading capital is, this is usually called capital at risk (CaR).

The capital at risk is the amount of capital the investor sets aside to cover up for any possible risk that might come up. The majority of times Capital at risk could even be used to pay losses and can also be used by some investors to get certain tax treatments. Now back to the 2% rule, while the investor is incorporating the capital at risk, he also has to incorporate the brokerage fees and any future fees that may arise. Stop-loss orders can also be used, so that the 2% rule can be effectively implemented.

The 2% rule is a range or limited parameter that guides investors while investing in a particular trade in order to stay within a specified risk management zone. Now let's look at an example of the 2% rule: suppose an investor has a trading account of $100,000 and decides to implement the 2% rule in a trade, he should risk nothing more than $2,000 or if he has an account of $25,000, he should risk nothing more than $500 in a trade that is (2% × $25,000). When the investor is able to calculate his capital risk, it will definitely help him to know the number of shares that can be purchased. Even in case he loses in 10 consecutive trades, he can only lose 20% of his investment.

2. TRADE RISK:

After the investor has calculated his account risk, the following thing to do is to place their stop-loss order which was extensively explained in the previous chapter. The trade risk is the difference between the entry price and the stop-loss order. For instance, suppose an investor wants to buy a stock at an entry price of $160 and sets the stop-loss order at $140. The trade risk would be $160 - $140, which is $20 per share. Just like I mentioned in the previous chapter, the stop-loss order is used to determine the position size, which is how the stop-loss order comes into play by determining the position size of an investment.

3. ACCURATE POSITION SIZE:

Remember that we calculated the investor's account risk to be $500 per share and trade risk to be $20 per share; these two factors will guide the investor while determining his accurate position size. Since the investor knows that he can only risk $500 per trade and he is risking $20 per share. To calculate the correct position size, the investor needs to simply divide the account risk which is $500 by the trade risk, which is $20, ie $500/$20 = $25. This means that $25 shares can be bought.

This is exactly how the account risk and trade risk can be used to determine the accurate position size for an investor or trader.

POSITION SIZING AND GAP RISKING

Position sizing and gap risking are very important to the investor, in the sense that even if the trader uses an accurate position sizing, he may still lose more than their specified account risk limit, which is a stock gaps below their stop-loss order.

GAP RISKING:

Gap risk occurs when a stock's price falls below than expected. A gap risk can be up or down where the price of the stock may go from a higher level to a lower one without trading in between. Things like this happen when there are bad news about a company, which may cause the stock's price to go lower from the previous price. A gap risk can be reduced by closing positions at the close of a trading day, by executing stop-loss orders on aftermarket trading platforms or by incorporating hedges just as you learnt earlier.

Now back to position sizing, if a company has a chance of increased volatility but their earnings and announcement, investors should halve their position size in order to reduce the gap risk as much as possible.

For example, we calculated the investors position size to be $25 per share, this means that in order to reduce the investors gap risk as much as possible, the

$25 has to be halved, ie $25/2 = $12.5. Therefore, the maximum amount of money an investor can invest is a trade and minimise gap risk is $12.5 depending on the investor's account.

DIVERSIFICATION AS A MUST

Just as you learnt earlier, diversification is one of the major strategies in risk management. Even non-swing trade investors cannot invest without diversifying their investments in order to minimise risks as much as possible. Here, you will be learning about various strategies and techniques that you can make use of when diversifying your trade.

Diversification is the key to a successful trade, "safe", secure and "smart" are three words that can be used to best describe diversification. Traders that diversify their trades know the benefit of diversification. In a lay man's terms, diversification simply means *"Don't put all eggs in one basket"*. Diversification means variety- investing in various trades so as to minimise risks in one trade alone. Diversifying is not only about trading in various markets, it is about diversifying how you see the market. When you do diversification in the right way, you will begin to see untapped opportunities in various markets. Diversity gives you more and better opportunities to trade while lowering the overall risk.

In order to be a good diversified trader, you have to focus on three components of diversification. These are entry strategy, exit strategy and money management. If you are asked this question, what kind of trader are you? Scalper, swing trader or trend trader? Now most persons will go for or categorise themselves under swing trading. Why didn't you go for scalper or trend trader? Why didn't you diversify into those categories of trading?

If you are able to diversify into the three categories mentioned- scalping, swinging and trending, you will be able to discover the best trade for the current market condition. And by looking into that trade that your market conditions set for you, it will definitely help you to be a more successful trader.

The average trader finds it is difficult to recognise why he makes so much losses, the average trade still has good trades and bad trades, but the bad trades outweighs the good trades, which is why he still makes so much losses. They just can't seem to understand their underlying problem. Successful traders understand that when they sync their trading system with their market, they make more money. But when they aren't sync, they lose money. It is just like trying to fit in a square peg in a round hole.

After the average trader has had huge losses, they get rid of that system and look for new ones. They repeat this cycle over and over again with the same result and until they learn to diversify their system and take advantage of their predominant market, that cycle will keep repeating itself.

How to diversify your system.

Diversifying your system should be done when you are willing to mitigate your risk. You begin diversification when you are able to recognise three market conditions: scalp, swing and trend. A better way of getting this done is by changing the time frames on you charts. For instance, you may use an hour to look for trend trades, a five minute chart to watch out for scalp trades and a fifteen minute chart to look out for swing trade. This method is much better than building a separate system for each market style.

When building your three signals for scalp swing and trend trade, *make sure that you are clear enough to make a reasonable decision.* You should be able to look at a chart and determine if you have a scalp, a swing or a trend.

The clarity of your signal is extremely essential for your success. In fact, some say that signal clarity is even more important than signal accuracy. Some traders think that they are not making money because their signal is not very accurate. This is because they have ignored the other two components, which are clearly money management and exit strategy. They lack diversification skills in the market. Some of them don't even know that if they have a good money management strategy and exit strategy, they can make more money. Even if their signal is 50/50.

Money management is simply about how you are able to efficiently manage the capital you invest in a particular trade and how you minimise risks and maximise returns despite the various market conditions and changes. Money management will require you to be very smart and alert in your market, looking out for trends, signals and peaks. The goal there is to strike when you are supposed to strike.

Your exit strategy should be determined as soon as you have clearly determined your signals. After you have clearly analysed your market and its conditions.

You should quickly begin your exit plan to avoid future losses.

You shouldn't be rational at all when it comes to your entry strategy. Before you choose to enter into a particular market you should do your market analysis properly to determine the possible benefits, trend analysis, market conditions, currency translations and market variations. This will help you get to know your market at your fingertips.

DIVERSIFICATION SYSTEMS

Diversification simply means that a trader should not rely on one approach to the various markets in front of him. Successful traders are the ones that are able to diversify by trading their stocks in different industries.

Diversification could be accomplished by practicing the following options. He can use different styles to the same market. A trader could take advantage of the price changes at some periods. He could also make use of some selling strategy by taking advantage of some flat periods in the market. Each of these techniques can be used simultaneously.

Another option would be trading by using the same strategy with different time frames or different markets. A discretionary trader can use that approach for uncorrelated markets while an algorithmic trader may use the same approach for different markets or he could trade different strategies with different markets. These diversification methods could be used to provide the desired diversification needed. The key to diversification is simply to trade multiple different ways.

CORRELATION IS THE DANGER

Correlation is defined as the reciprocal, parallel or complementary relationship between two or more comparable objects according to the English dictionary. Correlation considers the mutual relationship between two independent values. Traders use correlation to find out whether there is a relationship between two variables and what kind of relationships that exists between those two variables. In trading, -1 means that the correlation between two values are negative, 0 represents that no correlation exists between two variables, while 1 means that there is a positive correlation between the two of them.

As much as correlation is used in statistics to understand the relationship between two variables, it is also very much applicable in trading.

CORRELATION DEFINED

In trading, a correlation scale is usually used to measure or check the relationship between two or more values. The correlation measures from -1 to 1.

- -1 signifies that there is a negative correlation between two values, meaning that as A increases in value, B reduces or decreases in value and vice versa.

- 0 means that no form of relationship exists between the two values, one value is not dependent on the other one in any way.

- 1 implies that there is a positive correlation between A & B, that is, as A increases in value, B also increases in value simultaneously.

Sometimes there may be in between values, such as values greater than -0.8 or values less than 0.8, but they are not usually considered as significant. This scale is to measure correlation in trading.

Pearson's Correlation Coefficient

The Pearson's correlation coefficient is the formula that is used to calculate correlation, it was invented by the mathematician Karl Pearson.

For example, suppose we want to find the correlation between two values A & B, at a given period of time. First we need to calculate the average mean of each value, and after that, subtract the mean result from A & B respectively. Your result should be then added together, same thing applies to B. Each of your A and

B values should be multiplied together and then divided by the number of values you started with minus 1. That means, if you took your values over a 5-day period, you should divide by 4.

Standard deviation in trading is the difference between the value of a stock and its mean average over a period of time. Before being able to obtain the standard deviation of a value, you must first obtain your variance (which is not the same as covariance); you can obtain the variance by taking the values of a stock, A, over a period of time. As with covariance. The mean average of stock A, is calculated and then subtracted from each value. Their individual total is then squared and added together.

This total is then divided by the original amount of value minus 1 to give you the variance. The square root of the variance is the standard deviation. Thus, the correlation coefficient can be calculated by dividing the covariance of A and B by the sum of the standard deviations of A and B.

CORRELATION VERSUS COVARIANCE

It is of utmost necessity for traders to understand the difference between correlation and covariance. If the two are mistaken for each other, it can lead to confusion and mistakes. Covariance is used to measure the rate at which two values vary from each other. Meanwhile, correlation measures how much the difference between A and B is related. When these values are plotted on a graph page, the correlation value will stay closest to the mean than the covariance.

ADVANTAGES AND DISADVANTAGES OF CORRELATION

Advantages:

- A correlation graph can be used to display trends and is also used to determine the future direction of a value.

- Pearson' s formula can be used to calculate large quantities of data, which allows traders to calculate correlation over a long period of time.

- The correlation scale of -1 to 1 is very easy to understand even to those that are beginners in trading.

Disadvantages:

- Correlation cannot show whether the relationship between A and B was caused by a certain factor or not. Even a good correlation of -1 to 1 can't determine if the movement of A directly affects the movement of B or vice versa.

- As much as correlation can tell trends based on historical data, it cannot determine what will happen in the future. Even diversification of one's portfolio usually works by assumptions, that correlation coefficients must remain the same.

- Correlation usually measures a linear relationship, although, most times, two values that don't have a linear relationship might still have some correlation.

APPLICATIONS OF CORRELATION IN SWING TRADING

Here, you will be learning possible applications and uses of correlation. Let's proceed.

1. Correlation swaps:

This is a contract which promises a return for every increase in the correlation coefficient between two products. It is almost similar to pair trading.

2. Pairs trading:

This works by finding two securities that are highly historically correlated and tries to capitalise on any diversion from their correlation.

It works this way: a trader studies two values closely, finds the stocks that performs more A and the stock that performs lesser B. Afterwards, he checks for any deviation between both and once there is a diversion, the trader sells both at the same time. He makes profit by going short on A and long on B.

3. Portfolio protection & diversification:

Since every trader's goal is to make more profit and manage risks, he has to learn to protect and diversify his portfolio. They make use of correlation by securities, which have little or no correlation at all to their equities, they are like alternative investments that have no relationship at all with their main investments. The reason behind it is that, when one of the investment or equity depreciates in value, it won't affect the other equity that has no correlation at all.

4. Measuring the relative performance of two variables:

Traders make use of this method when they want to understand the type of correlation that exists between two variables in order to know which one to invest. A typical example of this can be seen in the negative correlation that exists between stocks and bonds. Investors will take advantage of the better market and invest there.

MOVING AVERAGES

Moving averages are one of the most widely used technical indicators that most traders use to trade in their various market. This is because they are very easy to use and apply. Despite the fact that they have been around for a long time, their uniqueness in being easy to be measured, tested, and applied makes them the absolute right choice for traders. Here, we will be looking at some key things that you have to know in order to become a successful trader.

- Simple moving averages
- Exponential moving averages

1. SIMPLE MOVING AVERAGES (SMA):

This is the average closing price of a security, over a specified period of time. Calculating the simple moving price of a security is not so complicated if you understand the formula. The simple moving price of a security is not just something for technical analysis but is also considered a formula used in engineering and mathematical studies.

Understand it this way, let's say, suppose the last five closing prices are 28.93 + 28.48 + 28.44 + 28.91 + 28.48 = 143.24

Now to calculate the simple moving average value, we have to divide the total closing prices by the number of periods.

Five-day SMA = 143.24/5 = 28.65

28.65 is the simple moving average value for that.

Note that this is only the mathematical aspect of SMA. Theoretically, there is an infinite number of simple moving averages. The most common simple moving averages that traders use are the 10, 20, 50, 100 and 200. These are five simple moving averages for the trader. If the simple moving averages are shorter, you will be receiving more signals when trading.

How can a trader apply the simple moving averages?

Here, I will be showing you some basic principles and rules that must be followed when applying simple moving average to your trade and how you can make more money with your simple moving average.

Now suppose you are going with the primary trend, apply the following.

- Seek stocks that are breaking down strongly.
- Apply the following SMAs 5, 10, 20, 40, 200 and get to see which of them contains the best price.
- After that, wait for the price to test the SMA and look for price confirmation that the stock is resuming direction at the primary trend.
- Input the trade on the next bar.

Using two simple moving averages fade out the primary trend.

1. Find stocks that are strongly breaking down.//
2. Choose two simple moving averages to apply to the chart.
3. Make sure that the price has not touched the 5 period SMA or 10 period SMA
4. Wait for the price to close above or below both moving averages in the opposite direction of the primary trend.
5. Input the trade on the next bar.

EXPONENTIAL MOVING AVERAGE

This is the most ancient form of technical analysis and thousands of traders use it as indicators. In fact, I can say that this is most effective moving average method that most traders use in various markets. Here, you will be learning how to make use of the exponential moving average and how you can apply it to your trade in order to become a more successful trader.

What is an exponential moving average?

The exponential moving average strategy is usually used to find out the predominant trend in the market. It is also used by most traders to provide a level of resistance and some support to implement and execute your trade. The EMA strategy works in all kind of markets, ranging from stocks, indices, forex, currencies and crypto-currencies market. You can even work with it on your preferred chart.

The exponential moving average is a line on the price chart that uses a formula to smooth out price action. It is used to calculate average price over a specific period of time. The exponential moving average focuses more on the current price, which means that it is more dependable because it responds faster to the current changes in price data.

The good thing about exponential moving average is that it tries to reduce confusion as much as possible. It also smoothens the price and shows the trend and is more dependable in forecasting future changes in the market price. Now suppose we want to calculate the exponential moving average value. We can make use of this formula.

EMA = {close − EMA (previous day)} × multiplier + EMA (previous day).

The rule is that if the price trades above the moving average, then we are in an uptrend as long as we are above the exponential moving average. At this point, we should expect higher prices. On the other hand, if we are trading below, we are in downtrend. Unless we trade below the moving average, we should expect lower prices.

EMA (trading rules − sell trade). The EMA technique is composed of two elements. The first thing to do to find out a new trend is to use 2 exponentially moving averages as an entry filter.

When you use one moving average with a greater period and one with a lesser period of time, you automate the strategy. In this process, subjectivity is removed from trading.

First step: plot the 20 and 50 EMA

Second step: wait for the EMA crossover and for the price to trade above the 20 and 50 EMA

Third step: wait for the zone between 20 and 50 EMA to be tested at least two times, they seek for possible buying opportunities.

Fourth step: buy at the market when retesting the zone between 20 and 50 EMA for the third step.

Fifth step: place the protective stop loss 20 pips below the 50 EMA

Final step: take profit once we break and close below the 50 EMA

Apply these rules and principles closely, and you are right on your way to become a successful trader in your market.

CASH AS POSITION

Cash position is the part of your investment portfolio assets that is cash or cash equivalents. It is usually checked through liquidity ratios. Even when a cash position provides liquidity reserves and helps making up for losses, it can earn a risk free rate of returns. An excessive accumulation of cash can be an opportunity cost. Cash drag is simply when an investor prefers having a portion of his portfolio as cash rather than investing it in the market.

The majority of traders prefer investing all their cash in the market because during periods of inflation, their cash position will yield negative returns. However, some investors might still decide to hold their cash at hand to pay for account fees and commissions. Here, we will be considering two aspects of cash position for traders:

- Cash trading
- Position trading.

CASH TRADING:

This is the buying and selling of securities by using capital to fund the transaction instead of the use of margin. Securities talk about a " financial instrument" that has some sort of monetary value. Security represents ownership position. While margin there refers to a loan gotten from a brokerage firm to buy an investment, it is actually the difference between the cash in a trader' s account and the one of a broker' s account.

Cash trading requires you to use the funds that are available in your account to pay for every transaction that you make. Sometimes, most brokers offer cash trading accounts to traders because it is much easier to open and maintain than margin accounts. When there is no margin, long term investors use this account as the best option because they don' t usually purchase securities on margin. Cash trading happens when a trader chooses to do transactions with a brokerage account or traders account, without the use of margins. Let's look at some key things to consider when trading with cash.

SETTLEMENT DATE:

This is the time when a transaction's deadline has reached and the buyer has to complete his payment. Stocks trades that are in cash accounts usually use three business days before it gets to the settlement date. Although it has been changed to two days, during settlement, securities are transferred to the buyer's account and the cash enters into the seller's account. Some common cash violations may include:

- Cash liquidation violation: here, you have to make sure that you have enough cash in your account to cover a trade.

- Free riding: this kind of violation resists investors from buying and selling securities before paying with their cash account.

- Good faith violation: this happens when a trade

purchases a stock with funds that haven't been settled yet and liquidates it before the settlement.

Cash trading still has some pros and cons in its system. The good thing about it is that it does not involve the use of margin as much as possible, which makes it very stress free. However, there is a lesser upside potential due to the lack of leverage.

POSITION TRADING

This is a trading strategy that happens when a trader holds a position in security for a very long time, usually in a number of months or years. Position traders don't focus on short-term price movements in favour of pinpointing and profiting from longer-term trends. This type of trading almost resembles investing. Position trading has one of the largest time frame out of all other existing trades. Even though it usually involves much risk, there is also a potential profit from it as well.

The benefits of position trading includes;

- Capitalisation of substantial trends.
- Reducing the market noise.
- Poor positions maintenance.

Strategies and techniques in position trading

Good traders make use of fundamental analysis and technical analysis to understand possible price trends in the market. Here, you are going to learn about some powerful techniques and strategies that will guarantee your success in trading:

1. Trading breakouts:

Position traders use trade breakout to find out the next major move in the market. Traders that make use of this technique are trying to open a position at the initial stage of a trend.

A breakout happens when a price of an asset goes out of a defined support or resistant level in an increased volume. The reason behind it is that it is best to open a position during the time when the security moves below the support level. For you to successfully trade breakouts, you have to have courage in finding out support and resistance periods.

2. Pullback strategy:

A pullback occurs when there is a little reversal change in the predominant price of a trend. This strategy is used when there is a long term trend in the market. These traders take advantage of those null periods in the market.

The sense behind this strategy is to purchase stocks at a lower price and sell them at a higher price before the market' s price is reversed. If this is successfully achieved, the trader won' t just profit from the trade but also avoid losses that may be caused by price reversal in the market.

3. Support and resistance trading:

Support and resistance levels in trading can show you the direction of an assets price in order to help you position your resources well. It can also tell you to either open or close a position in a particular assets. The resistance level shows that the price of a security cannot be able to break or fallout. This strategy requires traders to analyse chart patterns, identify resistance and support levels using the historic price of a security, indicate future levels and use technical indicator to provide a dynamic support and resistant levels.

SOME INSTRUMENTS THAT POSITION TRADERS USE FOR TRADING.

Here, I am going to mention some useful instruments that position traders make use of in trading. They include:

1. Shares CFD
2. Commodity CFD
3. Indices CFD
4. Forex CFD
5. Cryptocurrency CFD.

RISK/BENEFIT RATIO

The risk/reward ratio shows the investor the size of reward that he stands to gain for every dollar that he is willing to risk in an investment. The majority of investors and traders use this method to determine and calculate the total returns that an investment can bring to them and also the amount of risk associated with the investment.

Now let's try to understand this with a very practical example, suppose an investor wants to invest in a certain stock that cost $2 that has a reward of $10. This means he has to $2 for a potential reward $10 in the future. His risk/reward is 2:10; another investor that has a risk / reward ratio of 1:7 means that he is willing to risk $1 for a possible reward of $7 on a certain stock.

Good investors and traders use this technique to assess various trades in their options and know which one they should go for. The risk/reward ratio is normally calculated by dividing the amount of money an investor stands to lose or the amount of money an investor wants to use in investing by the prospective profits and rewards the trader or investor stands to gain.

How does the risk/reward ratio work?

Traders use the risk/reward ratio when trading with stocks in their trade. The average risk/reward ratio between several trading techniques may be different, although most traders prefer to use a trial and error method in order to determine the standard ratio for a given trading strategy. Most investors already have a specified ratio for any of their investments.

In some cases, traders find their ideal risk/reward ratio for their investments to be 1:3. However, investors and traders can manage their risk and rewards by using stop-loss orders.

Benefits of the risk/reward ratio in trading.

The risk/reward ratio teaches investors how to calculate their potential rewards for every risk they are going to make on any investment. The risk compares the difference between an entry point to a stop loss and a take profit order to provide the ratio of profit to loss.

Stop loss orders is usually in conjunction with the risk reward ratio to help minimise losses and manage investments. Just like you saw earlier, the role of stop-loss order is to signal the selling of a portion of a trader' s portfolio when it gets to a specified lower level. Most investors use their brokerage accounts to place their stop-loss orders without having any extra costs attached to it.

How to calculate the risk/reward ratio of any investment.

When actively using the risk/reward ratio in investments you begin to discover that most times good investments are very difficult to find. Here, you will be learning how to calculate the risk/reward ratio in any investment and how to incorporate it into your investment. Let's take a look at the ABC method.

The ABC method:

Now suppose you do your research very well and you find out that company ABC's stock is a stock you will like to invest in. The ABC stock worth $25, while some time ago it was $29. In your thoughts, you decide to believe that in the future this ABC stock will go up to $29, thus being able to profit you $4 for each stock you decide to purchase and therefore you finally decide to purchase the stock. You have $500 in your account and decided to purchase 20 shares.

Now, most investors can be very sentimental about this and quickly decide to purchase the 20 shares without even calculating their risk/reward ratio for each stock they may decide to purchase. It is important to note that this can lead to huge losses in the future in case the trade doesn't turn out as planned. That's why as a good trader, you have to understand how and when the risk/reward ratio. As a good trader, don't be rational and sentimental about it by purchasing the 20 shares immediately without calculating your risk/reward ratio first. Now to calculate our risk/reward ratio for the ABC stock, since you finally decided to purchase 20 shares, $29 for each share will profit you $4 for 20 shares that will be the number of shares you want to purchase multiplied by your possible profit. For example, 20 × 4 = $80. After so much negotiation with the seller, you decide to purchase the 20 shares with $500. Therefore, to calculate your risk/reward ratio from this scenario, you should divide your reward from the 20 shares which is $80 by your total capital $500, $80/$500 = 0.16. This means that your risk/reward ratio for this particular trade is 0.16. Now I want you to analyse this value critically, is it a low risk/reward ratio or not? Will investors want to go for an investment like this? Is it worth it? It is highly recommended to take your time and think critically about these questions and answer them in your mind before moving to the next paragraph.

Have you answered and thought on those questions carefully? Let's proceed to the answers. Firstly, is it a low ratio or not? Remember I mentioned that most traders use their ideal risk/reward ratio as 1:3, which is 0.33 in decimal; suppose we decide to go with this, that means we should be comparing 0.33 with our 0.16. Now answer it yourself, is it low? YES.

Will investors...? NO, certainly most investors won't go for that kind of investment. Is it worth your investment? Hmmm...that will depend on you to answer. With this practical example, I hope you are now able to understand what the risk/reward ratio is all about.

Follow these steps if you really want to apply the risk/reward ratio to your trade;

1. Research on a stock and choose the best option.
2. Check your upside and downside targets based on current price.
3. Calculate your risk/reward ratio.

4. If the ratio is too low for your target, raise your downside target to try to get to an acceptable ratio.

5. If you haven't gotten an acceptable ratio yet, then try out a different investment idea.

CHAPTER 10
THE SKILL YOU NEED YO ACHIEVE YOUR FINANCIAL INCOME

The truth is that not every trader you see out there has what it takes to become a successful master trader in their trade. Becoming a very successful trader takes more than just waking up in the morning, analysing your charts, spotting for swings and thinking of new ways to improve, minimise losses and maximise profits.

To become a very successful trader in your niche, there are some very crucial and essentials things you need to consider about your market. You need to have some knowledge of fundamental economics, behavioural economics, financial markets and technical analysis. Even after acquiring that kind of knowledge, most traders might still not be able to qualify as successful master traders in their niche. What do you do then? The solution lies in following these skills and techniques that master traders use to achieve their financial income. I am going to explain powerful and proven skills that master traders apply in their trade. You must know the secrets of most traders to succeed in your trade.

1. RESEARCH AND ANALYSIS:

Even outside the trading world, the ability to carry out a quality and extensive research on a topic is a skill on its own. Researchers are paid heavily for their service. The same thing applies in trading, your ability to carry a quality and extensive market research gives you a leverage over the next trader in your niche. Just like the phrase goes "knowledge is power" ; this phrase has a long way to apply to the success of your trade. Your ability to understand and rediscover your market, trends, downsides and upsides lies on how well you do your research and analysis.

Successful traders are the ones that are skilled in

researching information that are relevant to their securities. What makes it so special is their ability to learn and act by utilising market information in their trade.

Master traders apply their analytical skills in spotting out trends and utilising the information. Even when it is applied in price action charts of various time frames.

When you do your market analysis as a trader, even as you identify unique trends and patterns, it is also very important to find out the approaches that are used in technical trading. It is definitely better to focus more on the best action to take than the money to make. When focusing on your market rather than your money, it will help you make good objective trading decisions to work with, doing that will help you build the most profitable trade for yourself. Focus on your trade and market rather than your potential income.

2. ADJUSTING YOUR MARKET ANALYSIS DUE TO CHANGING MARKET CONDITIONS:

Master traders don't stop researching on new market strategies and trading techniques, they make use of these strategies in various markets several times. When you combine all these techniques, there is certainly no doubt that they are good technical indicators that signal high probability trades. However, a good trader still has to learn a new skill of being able to adapt their trading techniques and strategies according to various market conditions so that ends can meet. Pay close attention to market signals that need you to adapt or change your strategy to be a master trader.

3. STAYING IN THE GAME:

Staying in the game is a skill that most traders find it difficult to learn no matter how much they try to learn. In a lay man's terms, staying in the game means playing the game "maturely". Every move you make is highly sacrosanct in determining the success or failure of your game. Even in other business worlds, the majority of business men are faced with peaks and "rock bottom" times. Or simply good times and bad times when they make loads of profit and times when they make little or no profit. Your courage and integrity to keep playing is what makes you a master trader. It's like the game of chess, sometimes you win, sometimes you lose, sometimes you learn but no matter what lies ahead you keep playing.

Most times, there are some trades you may take that can make you react in a very rational or sentimental way, those are times when the price action in the market goes in your favour and there are also times when the price action does not favour and you feel like closing off and quitting a trade. What master traders do in such situations is to keep staying in the game because they understand that the worst that can happen in any trade they take on is that they can either win from a trade, lose or learn from the mistake of a trade. Keep these three words in the game.

4. RECORD KEEPING:

Becoming a master trader isn't easy at all, it requires you to be able to overcome your trading emotions and act the right way. Record keeping is a skill that master traders use a lot of times. You aren't a successful trader if you haven't learnt how to keep record and notes on how their past trades went.

In fact, most master traders have what they call a "trading journal". This, enables them to take note and records of past trades, it is just like an appraisal to them. It records your entry point and your reason for buying or selling, placement of stop-loss order, take-profit orders, how you reacted to the market action and the level of your winning or losing.

A trade helps you to look back at what you did not do well in the past to improve or to remember how well you did in the past and keep doing it.

Every trader needs to master these skills if they really want to succeed in their trade, it is not just about mastering it, but also applying it in their trades to produce more profits. Become a skilled master trader today and you are heading towards the right path in becoming one of the best master traders in the swing trading market today.

CHAPTER 11
HOW TO FIND TRANSITIONS IN SWING TRADING

Let's think about this question; when should I trade a stock? Is the most frequently asked question in any trading platform, which is asked by both beginners and experts alike. This is because nobody wants to trade at the wrong time and thus loose money. Finding transitions in swing trading is very important just like it is important in any other strategy for trading. However, I think it's more crucial to be able to find transitions in swing trading because it will determine how long you should hold a stock and when exactly you need to let go so as to make your profits.

Transitions are simply the downtrend and uptrend movement of stocks in a given period of time. This movement can be tricky and can happen in several ways; stocks can fall precipitously. For example, it can also just turn on a dime either upward or downward. However, no matter the direction of the transition, you can still make your gains as far as you are able to recognise the transition early enough and make the right decision. This is exactly where a lot of people find it difficult; finding transitions. To successfully swing trade, you have to be able to recognise transitions. So in this part, I am going to explain a number of strategies I use to find transitions while trading.

To find transitions in swing trading, you have to constantly be on the lookout for a number of price patterns that occur from time to time in trades. The price patterns are identified with the help of a series of trend lines and curves; here are two basic types of pattern; the reversal and the continuation patterns. I would like to warn you that even if some of these patterns have been proven for a long time by traders and a lot of profits have been met by so many traders by maximising them, it doesn't mean that there is zero impossibility of failing at any time. With the right knowledge anyways, you will make more money than you will lose with these strategies. So let's look at them now, starting from the continuation pattern which signals a continuation of a bullish or bearish trend.

The cup and handle patterns

As stated by the name, the cup and handle pattern is an uptrend pattern that has a cup like formation. This pattern forms as a result of a halt in an uptrend that later form a peak and then a little retracement down again that now forms the cup handle. To track and easily identify the cup and handle patterns, you have to be able to keep track of past uptrends, because the cup start forming from a 15% to 50% dip from the peak of the uptrend. Then, it rises again to get to or very close to the peak where it started dipping from before; it slants down a little again to form the cup handle. An important thing you should note is that the handle side of this pattern should look like a very narrow price range that can be contained inside by two parallel lines. Sometimes, it takes the shape of a smaller rounded bottom.

Triangle trading patterns

This is a very popular continuation patterns among traders. The triangle pattern forms when price action changes in a series of lower highs and higher lows. To easily spot out this pattern, you have to watch out for a strategic upward movement of the trend line from the bottom and a downward movement of a top trend line within a specific period of time. This pattern can form with a minimum of two hits on the uptrend and downtrend respectively.

You must take note also that, the break of the triangle pattern is the most important aspect of the pattern. And the break can go either ways; downtrend or uptrend. This means you have to trade cautiously. However, the break out is predictable when you know the different types of triangle patterns. For instance, the ascending triangles, which often shows a flat upper trend and a rising lower trend most likely suggest a higher breakout while the descending triangles with a flat lower trend and descending upper trend tilts towards a lower breakout. The most difficult thing to predict is the symmetrical triangle, it doesn't really give a hint on the breakout direction.

Flags

This is another continuation pattern to look at. The flag pattern is formed with two parallel trend lines that can slope in the four primary directions. A halt in downtrend market forms an upward slope, while a flag with a downward slope points to a break in an uptrend market. When price breaks out of the flag formation, the market witnesses an increase in volume.

Heads and shoulders

This is a reversal pattern. Reversal patterns show a change in direction of any prevailing trend. The heads and shoulders pattern, as the name goes, has the shape of a head joined with shoulders and it can be seen at the market tops and market bottoms respectively. This pattern forms as a result of three different pushes in the market. The first push comes with an initial rice or peak in price, after this push comes a second push that outweighs the first and then the last push that looks exactly like the first one.

Like I mentioned earlier, this is a reversal pattern, so if an uptrend is interrupted by this pattern it most likely becomes a downtrend and vice versa when it interrupts a down trend. As a result, volume may increase or decrease at the break of a head and shoulder pattern depending on which trend it got interrupted.

Moving average crossovers

The moving average tool is an important tool swing traders use to monitor or find transitions. This tool helps traders to reduce the noise on the market price charts since, with the help of the average tool, we can state where the price of stocks is moving towards. If the moving average is up, then it means that the price of stocks is moving up, it means the opposite if it is pointed down. Then if it is moving sideways, it points most likely to a price range. You can adjust the moving average to any time frame of your choice. This tool can also be used as a support and resistance in upward and downward trends respectively.

CHAPTER 12
10 ENTRY STRATEGIES

Trading is not something you do absent minded or carelessly, unless of course you are prepared to lose all your money. If not, then you have to up your game and be more careful and one of the ways I am going to help you trade more carefully with and win more is by showing you ten awesome trade strategies that work right now. With these strategies you will maximise your wins and minimise your loss.

Trade entry strategies vary in different trade platforms and chart patterns, so you cannot really use the strategy you used for a particular trade pattern for a different one. Because of this, I have gathered up ten different entry strategies that apply to the different price chart patterns.

Identify swing points

In my opinion, this is the first and basic entry strategy. You have to first identify swing points before you make any move at all. Swing point is basically a pattern that has three candles. The basic rule while identifying swing points goes as follows: if you want to go on long positions then watch out for a swing point low, and then vice versa when you want to go on short positions.

Trade on consecutive price patterns

This is another basic entry strategy. Before you enter into any trade you should look at the how consecutive and consistent the price pattern has been. With this strategy you have to always consider the consecutive down days before a swing point low, if you want to go on the long side. If you are going on the long side, consider the consecutive up days before a swing point high. Also, make sure to keep your eyes on the support and resistant area of stocks to effectively use this strategy.

Aggressive swing point entry strategy

This strategy is riskier than the two entry strategies mentioned above, but of course the riskier it gets the more potential profits is possible to make. With this strategy, you go in or out on a stock before it swings low or high. You don't have to wait for any swing point to fully develop, you just buy in anticipation.

Cup and handle entry strategy

I explained the cup and handle pattern in the previous chapter. The ultimate rule to enter this pattern is to wait for the confirmation where the price breaks above the handle to enter the trade, the resistance that defines the handle structure should be your guide here. You can also enter the trade on the breakout of the initial peak where the cup started taking shape from.

The triangle pattern entry strategy

The triangle chart pattern is another important and common pattern that people should take into consideration to know how to enter the trade.

Generally, you should enter trade in a triangle pattern when the price breaks. If the break out is bullish, enter when the price closes above the upside trend line.Enter when the trade close below the downside trend line when the breakout is bearish. For you to time well, you have to keep a watch on the breakout candle, monitoring the candle will also reduce risks for you.

Head and shoulder entry strategy

The head and shoulder pattern is another important one just like many others. Basically, to enter a trade in this pattern you need to wait for the candle to close below the support level. Another entry strategy is to wait for the retest of the neckline as new resistance. Entering at this point, will help reduce the risk.

T-30 chart pattern entry strategy

This is an entry strategy where you watch out for the T-30 pattern; a kind of tail that goes down through the 30 period exponential moving average. The T-30 pattern resembles a hammer candle stick pattern on your chart. In order to entry the strategy for this pattern you need to go in or purchase a stock on the day of the hammer (you will see it on your chart) when you see the stock is at support level and the volume is high. Just in case you are not able to trade during the day, then simply place your buy stop a little bit above the high on the hammer day.

The side trap pattern entry strategy

The side trap pattern is a very deceitful pattern like the name states; it is a trap. And a lot of traders lose their money here because they make the wrong derivations and as a result make the wrong moves in the built up of this pattern. The wrong moves made by traders, result to the completion of this pattern, which highly profits the traders that made the right choices.

The method to enter the side trap and take your profits is by taking a position with the stock on the day of the reversal candle. However, don' t make the mistake of trading about any reversal candle. Ensure that the candle you are trading on closes more than halfway into the range of the candle break down. Anything less than this would mean the reversal candle is weak and it will definitely be a wrong move to make.

The abc or swing trap pattern entry strategy

This pattern is a tricky one too where prices seems to be going up and then pulls back again which entraps traders and especially the ones who are long on stocks. The majority of them go out of trade which now makes the price rise again.

The best way to enter this pattern is to allow a candlestick pattern to develop on the final swing of the pattern and then buy your stock on the day the candles stick pattern shows up. Another option would be to place your buy stop above the high of the candle pattern.

Ghost town pattern entry strategy

Stocks have low volatility whenever you see this

pattern. You will notice a lot of pullbacks into the TAC and end in narrow range candles. There are three basic ways you can enter this pattern. These are:

1. Place your buy stop above the high of the highest narrow range candle.

2. You can also wait for another pattern to develop before you enter stock

3. The entry is difficult because the stocks are hard to predict in this pattern but then making use of the sixty minute chart is always helpful, since it warns you of potential breakout. In order to properly enter this pattern, move down a time frame to the 60 minute chart while you wait for the breakout.

CHAPTER 13
10 EXIT STRATEGIES

Knowing when to get out of a trade is very important. A lot of traders actually go into a trade, make their profits but stay longer on the trade after that and pay for it by losing all the profits they already made. The swing exit strategies I'm going to be showing you will help you get out of a trade when it favours you and when it doesn't.

Also, keep in mind that there is no such thing as a perfect strategy. Exist strategy vary and are limited to particular trade strategies, just like the entry strategies I just showed you. So we will just go from the basic strategies to the ones suited for specific patterns.

Set your initial stop loss order

Setting your initial stop loss order at the exact moment when you buy a stock will safeguard your capital in case the market goes wrong. A stop loss order closes a trade for you by getting you out of it. I will also advice that you do your research well so that you will know the right place to set your stop loss order.

Use trailing stops

Another simple way to exit a trade is by using trailing stops strategy. With this strategy, you can easily pocket the amount of profits that you can make from a very comfortable position and successively exit the trade. To use this in a typical swing trade that has a holding period of 2-5 days, trail your stops to 10 – 15 cents. Place at the lowest between the low of the previous day and the current low. You are able to change or adjust your trails depending on how long or short you want to go; it all depends on your general trading plan and strategy.

Trend line exit strategy

Using the trend line as an exit strategy is another good and simple exit strategy. As an advice, it hugely depends on your trend line when the trade you are on has a clearly defined trend movement. In this way you will be able to draw a very clear and simple trend line. The break of a clear trend line is always a good time to leave a trade.

The resistance strategy

The resistance level is a very important term or concept in trading. In simple words, it is the price at which an asset meets pressure on the way due to the number of traders who want to sell at that particular price. The resistance of level of a stock helps us to identify when is time to exit a trade. For example, the first resistance area a stock will face will be at the previous swing point high. If the pullback trade you bought doesn' t look good at that point, then you should exit the trade.

Head and shoulder exit strategy

The best time to exit a trade in the head and shoulder pattern is when the neckline has been immediately penetrated. When this happens then it is okay to exit.

You can also place your stop below the right shoulder. Placing the stop at the head of the pattern is another strategy to exit too, but it is a bit riskier.

Cup and handle exit strategy

The price of stock swings up and down around the handle of the cup most times and traders might get confused on where to place their stop order and exit. If that's the question on your mind, the solution to this problem is to place your stop order on the recent swing low. It is much safer there.

Run from the trade if the stop-loss is below the half way point of the cup. If the stop loss is placed wrongly, you will loose. In this pattern, the stop loss should always be around the upper third of the cup because the handle always occurs around the upper half of the cup.

Fixed reward to exit targets

This is a very simple exit strategy. In this strategy, the distance from the point of entry to the place you will put your stop loss is considered as one unit of risk. With this strategy, your plan will be to take multiple profits based on the count and then exit the trade once you've made that amount of profits. The strategy helps traders not to get carried away with the profits without knowing when to exit the trade.

The breakout Triangle pattern exit strategy

This strategy can work in all the types of triangle. With this strategy, you exit a trade when an asset drops below the lower trend line of the triangle so as to take as many profits as you can as the price breaks out of the triangle. If you notice that the price is breaking out, simply place your stop loss above the upper trend line or above the recent swing high. You can also use a profit target by targeting it at a price equal to the entire height of the triangle.

The bottom- top exit strategy

The bottom-top is an advanced analysis strategy that might require some time to master. This strategy focuses on making a major high profit before exiting a trade. But to use it, a trader must have a good sense of judgment to be able to call the highs and lows and then the failed retest. However, in order to use this strategy successfully you must obey the golden rule which is the following: the longer the price takes to fail, the more decisive the failure is.

The best way to use this strategy is to wait before making a major high, and then wait for a pullback immediately after the major high. Then finally wait for the failed attempt to break that high. Once this happens, it is a god time to exit the trade.

Fundamental analysis

I am reporting this as last because you shouldn't really depend on fundamental analysis for trading, especially when entering any trade. But then, fundamental analysis is useful because it can tell you which currency pair or stock will move and which one will fall. This can make you plan an exit or exit a trade. Fundamental analysis works better in exiting trades than in entering them. I advise people to always combine fundamental analysis with any other analysis I mentioned above before taking any final decision.

CHAPTER 14
WHAT YOU WILL NEVER HAVE TO DO – THE BIG MISTAKES

One thing I am sure every trader has successfully done as a beginner and even as an expert is to make mistakes. We are all bound to make mistakes at one point or another during trading and most times we pay for it, but then we also learn from our mistakes. There are several possible mistakes a trader can make, but right now I'm going to take you through some of the common mistakes that traders have made that you shouldn't make if you haven't done it already.

Don't allow external factors to mislead you

As a swing trader, looking at the external influencer of a particular stock and making your decisions based on their activity is extremely risky. You should make your decisions based on the actual price of a stock at the moment instead of the expected price of the stock due to its fundamentals. Taking such things in consideration might work in long term trades but not in swing trade, since you don't hold stocks for too long to allow the their fundamentals to play out to your benefit.

Looking at stock fundamentals can distract you from the real thing. Avoid it and trade with actual price of stocks at the moment.

Don't get carried away by profits

This is a mistake a lot of beginners make, and it is a very costly one. I fell victim of this mistake a lot of times as a beginner and the cost of this mistake hit me with a shock always. As I result of that, I make sure I warn all my students continuously of this danger.

Focusing more on managing risks than on making profits you won't only reduce the losses, but you will also make more profits than just focusing on making money. Swing trade is more about managing risks than focus on gains. This might not sound so good to you, but the truth is when my eyes are looking for risks to avoid and manage, I find more ways to make profits too, and when I am all focused on making profits, I rarely see the drawbacks, I fall into them and lose more than I ever gained. Stay away from these mistakes.

Chasing top and bottom is risky

One of the most amazing things that can happen to a trader is to rightly pick the tops and bottom in the market. I have had that luck few times, and that it is all it is, luck. The reality is that no trader knows unarguably when a trade will swing to the top or to the bottom. Trying to always predict it and act accordingly is a very risky thing to do, and so, you must avoid it. In swing trade try to stay with what market charts and patterns and be comfortable with a modest return of about 5% to 10%.

Don't fall for the Holy Grail myth

Some traders actually believe that there is a holy grail somewhere. By Holy Grail I mean that there is a perfect system that gives you 100% assurance of profits and no risk at all. Many traders have fallen for this myth and tried to find it by using some stock trading program. I can assure you that if you go along this line you will lose a whole lot of money. If there is a holy grail, there wouldn't be a market at all, since the losses that people face are part of the market.

Don't make any move you didn't spend time to analyze

Again, beginners fall for this pitfall in swing trading. Don't make the mistake of being a blind swing trader. You must be able to see the whole picture before making any move. The mistake a lot of traders make is to trade on every little opportunity they perceive, without really thinking of other factors and how their move can fail and crash just after few minutes of making them.

As a rule, make a trade move only when the odds are in your favor not when it is appealing. For you to know if the odds are favorable, you have to study the charts well instead of making small uncalculated moves.

Don't over trade

Trading takes discipline and commitment. If you lose these two qualities along the way I bet you will pay for it. A lot of traders get carried away without considering the entry and exit criteria they already set prior to any trade. This happens mostly when they are gaining a lot from the market and so they forget when to let go of a trade. You don't have to let go of a trade when you start losing; obey the signs when you see them and stop hoping that the trade would still turn around in your favor. Remember take as little risk as possible and not be greedy.

Don't go short on an uptrend stock

This is another common mistake people make. I have made it in the past: I thought that a trade was bad and there was no way it could maintain a consistent rise. So, I started going short on it only to see it rise after a while, to the point where people actually made a lot of money from it. Uptrend stocks will always rise higher even when your emotions don't agree with them. Don't go short on uptrend, you will lose.

CHAPTER 15
A SUCCESS STORY

I can't really say who or where I first heard of trading. Some years ago a friend, and colleague of mine, persuaded me to start trading. I was skeptical at first because I thought it would be a gamble but then, after some persuasion from him, I learnt the basics and decided to start with it.

Whenever my friend hears me tell this story, he always points out the fact that it was not his persuasive abilities that made me join trading, but the fact that I was becoming poorer than I wanted to admit. I'm too proud to admit it in front of him, but I will tell the truth right here, just for you. I was speedily getting broke; the salary I was earning at that point in my life was not even enough for my daily needs. It was so bad; then I started thinking about my colleague that was doing real well and we were working in the same place. That changed everything. I put down my doubts and fears and decided to plunge in into trading.

He advised me to start out buying breakouts, so as I did. But I didn't have much success on it, the stocks always moved against me. I got discouraged, but I decided to keep on going and try other strategies that might turn out well for me. So, at that point I had to sell of the little properties I had; I sold my old tired truck that I inherited in order to fund my account with $2000.

During this period, I spent some time studying about swing trading, I joined trade chat groups and learnt a lot of things from my friend. So, I started to swing trading with a lot of obscure and relatively unknown products for some time and made a good amount of profits. Then I moved from trading obscure products to really popular stocks. The first popular stock I ever traded, which I made real profit from, was Amazon. Then I kept trading on popular stocks.

I learnt quite early that finding a trade niche will make

you more successful in trading and so I began to focus on technology stocks, although I still made moves on other types of stock. And then, as a beginner, I was buying at most four different stocks since I didn't have a lot of money and I was still slow at gathering and analyzing a lot of data that comes with trading on these stocks. So, I didn't want to put a lot of pressure on myself and make mistakes.

I started making more cash with swing trading, even though I had not mastered the whole strategy. That motivated me to be more knowledgeable about it. Not too long ago, I made some cool cash closing out my position on the telsa shares I had. I bought about 182 shares on Telsa at an average purchase price of 275.66$ and ended up selling my position at about 279.26$, making about six hundred and fifty-four-dollar net profits.

Actually, the credit of this trade should go to one of the trade chat group I was on, they pitched the trade to me. So, I entered the trade about two times, but then it was not really going as smoothly as planned because the stock was going up and down, so I decided to find the right time to close out on the trade.

I noticed the rejection and resistance that was happening with the stock was like a pattern. For about two to three months it was selling off, push up and then gets rejected; it was like a cycle. And one of the things I learnt before then was never to make any move on swing trade out of emotion, or any other factor that is not derived from what the charts are saying. When it has to do with selling out especially, I learnt to make my decisions by looking at the patterns of trend of the stock I'm trading on.

So, I noticed the trend on Telsa by observing the 180 day 4-hour chart. I looked at other patterns, and the overall ones were showing that Telsa was making lower lows and lower highs. And it was descending at that moment, so I decided to close out with that stats and make profits instead of holding on to a trade that was fluctuating so much and I wasn't sure of how down it was going or how up it would have rose. I took this decision since, as I said, I was taught to make my moves in the market with the stats on the trends and patterns. Taking this position for all my trades have reduced risk for me and increased my profits over the years.

Till today I still thank and appreciate my friend for pushing me into trading; the truth is that it really changed my life for good. I earn more than I ever imagined just swing trading and it still gives me a lot of free time to do other things I want to do. Making the decision to not just trading, but to swing trade is like the best financial decision I have ever made in my life.

CHAPTER 16
A STORY OF RUIN

I already mentioned that I was always skeptical about trading before I finally decide to start trading. My skepticism was given by the fear of losing all of the little cash I still had in that period. Finally I was forced to make that decision, and thank God I did it. One of the things that I was taught and warned about was that, no trader and no strategy can ever give you, or promise you, zero percent risk and 100% profit. And, in fact, if you look for such strategy, run for your life because it will surely fail

There is no holy grail in trading; every trader suffers loss at one point or the other while trading. I have suffered myself some terrible losses. At the beginning of my trading career one of the problems I had was impatience. I was so impatient that I was almost glued to the chart screens at a point. I will enter a trade and not let it breath, instead I will keep monitoring and checking the little changes that was happening in the market. This led me to make so many wrong moves, every time I was seeing a little twist in the market and I was not giving it time to develop. I was then making a move and, most of the times It was the wrong one, making me lose out of the market.

Once, someone recommended me a stock, so I got long on it and decided I was going to play with the person' s strategy and make as many profits as possible. But then, I started watching the market too closely and at some point, the price fell slightly, I thought it was a bad stock and that it was going to keep falling. My conclusions were not based on any analysis at all and I was not seeing the whole picture of the market. I abandoned the strategy we were supposed to be trading with, and bailed out of the trade the next day. I bailed out when the price was at $3.8 only to see the price of the stock rise so high three days later. I had lost money while the guy that played with the strategy smiled to the bank.

I made this type of mistakes several times when I traded with my emotions and paid dearly for it. I played mostly with my emotions and not with numbers and patterns.

I made mistakes of trusting new products, that were released by one of the local companies around, to really be a good stock and rise so high, since I had been watching their activities for a while. I bought the stocks because of their potentials, but then a bigger company released the same type of products a week later and the company I bet on, crashed. I lost my money. I learnt my lesson and I stopped buying outside of what the numbers and charts are saying in the present.

But then, as Improved as a swing trader and made more money, I had a new problem. I was always so carried away by my profits that I didn't know when too exit a trade, losing a lot of money. I would buy a stock and watching it go up so high to inevitably pull back and become a downtrend, losing then all the money I made, including the capital. One of the most painful ones was an uptrend stock I bought for about $10,000, after a week I was up close to $23,000.35. It was a nice stock, I was happy, and I was expecting it to rise some more. And so, instead of looking at the charts to know when I should sell, I held on to the stock foolishly ignoring my exit strategies. I just woke up one morning to find out that the stock had pulled back so much that I lost all the money I made, and a part of my capital as well.

Another failure that comes strong to mind in my trading career was when I lost a lot of money on VRX because it dropped about %40 in a day. I would have saved myself a lot of money if I had followed the chart and exit the trade quickly, but then, I thought the stock would have raised with the same speed it fell, and I should have held on. But to my disappointment, it never really rose. I lost thousands on this stock. I learnt that the more money you make and invest the costlier mistakes becomes and so the more careful you should be.

Like I just said, the more money you make and invest, the costlier mistakes become. When I learnt this, I made a decision to be very careful not to repeat a particular mistake. But the thing is that you can really never trade on zero risks and loss. What you can do is to minimize risk and maximize profits. I have had more success than failures in my swing trading journey and anybody can have as much success, and even better, than I have had. All you have to do is to play with the rules and minimize the risk.

CONCLUSION

How badly do you want it? What you learnt here does not make you an expert, neither a professional. You have to go and practice a lot, and I promise you, you will fail too – because most times the map varies from the terrain. Another thing you should note is that, sometimes nothing is wrong with this map but it might be the way you read the map and, in this case, the map is this book. I strongly advise you to get a mentor. They will stand beside you and guide you through the troubled waters.

Do you want to become a swing trading expert? Then go and practice – go and do something with what you have read here, otherwise this would be just another book on the shelf. Books do not make people, decisions that are backed up with consistent actions do.